Desire Lines

Also by Barry MacSweeney

The Boy from the Green Cabaret Tells of His Mother (Hutchinson, 1968; McKay, 1969)
The Last Bud (Blacksuede Boot, 1969)
Joint Effort, with Pete Bland (Blacksuede Boot, 1969)
Flames on the Beach at Viareggio (Blacksuede Boot, 1970)
Our Mutual Scarlet Boulevard (Fulcrum, 1971)
12 Poems and a Letter, with Elaine Randell (Curiously Strong, 1971)
Just 22 and I Don't Mind Dyin': The Official Poetical Biography of Jim Morrison, Rock Idol (Curiously Strong, 1971; Turpin, 1973)
Brother Wolf (Turret, 1972)
Fools Gold (Blacksuede Boot, 1972)
Five Odes (Transgravity Advertiser, 1972)
Dance Steps (Joe DiMaggio, 1972)
Six Odes (Ted Kavanagh, 1972)
Fog Eye (Ted Kavanagh, 1973)
Far Cliff Babylon (Writers Forum, 1978)
Black Torch (New London Pride, 1978)
Odes (Trigram, 1978)
Blackbird (Pig Press, 1980)
Starry Messenger (Secret Books, 1980)
Colonel B (Colin Simms, 1980)
Jury Vet: Odes (Bath Place, 1981)
Ranter (Slow Dancer, 1985)
The Tempers of Hazard, with Thomas A. Clark and Chris Torrance (Paladin, 1993)
Hellhound Memos (Many Press, 1993)
Pearl (Equipage, 1995)
Zero Hero, in *etruscan reader III* (etruscan, 1996)
The Book of Demons (Bloodaxe, 1997)
Postcards from Hitler (Writers Forum, 1998)
Pearl in the Silver Morning (Poetical Histories, 1999)
Sweet Advocate (Equipage, 1999)
False Lapwing (Poetical Histories, 2002)
Wolf Tongue: Selected Poems 1965-2000 (Bloodaxe, 2003)
Horses in Boiling Blood (Equipage, 2004)

Prose

Elegy for January: A Life of Thomas Chatterton (Menard, 1970)
Interviewed by Eric Mottram, *Poetry Information*, No. 18 (1978)
'The British Poetry Revival, 1965-79', *South East Arts Review* (1979)
Letters and other writings in *Certain Prose of the English Intelligencer*,
    ed. by Neil Pattison, Reitha Pattison, and Luke Roberts (Mountain, 2012/2014)

Barry MacSweeney

Desire Lines
Unselected Poems 1966-2000

Edited by Luke Roberts

Shearsman Books

First published in the United Kingdom in 2018 by
Shearsman Books
50 Westons Hill Drive
Emersons Green
BRISTOL
BS16 7DF

www.shearsman.com

ISBN 978-1-84861-579-3

Copyright © The Estate of Barry MacSweeney, 2018

The right of Barry MacSweeney to be identified as the author of this work
has been asserted by his Estate in accordance with the
Copyrights, Designs and Patents Act of 1988.
All rights reserved.

Introduction and editorial matter copyright © Luke Roberts, 2018

Contents

Acknowledgements	10
Introduction	11

from **The Boy from the Green Cabaret Tells of his Mother** (1968)

The autobiography of Barry MacSweeney	21
To Lynn at Work Whose Surname I Don't Know	22
On the Gap Left After Leaving	23
Walk	24
The Track, Fervour	26
Sealine	27
Bladder Wrack Blues	27
A Letter, This Far Away, Tonight for Liberty	28
One Year Old, The Wilted Hybrid	29
& The Biggest Bridge is Forty Feet Long	30
On the Burning Down of the Salvation Army Men's Palace, Dog Bank, Newcastle	31
The Axe	32
The Boy from the Green Cabaret Tells of His Mother	33
The Copper Heart	34
City	35
Song	35
Pastoral	36
2nd Telephone Song	36
The Decision, Finally (for Jeremy Prynne) 4 a.m., March 24 Sparty Lea	37
To Me Mam, Somewhere to the North of This Shit	38

from **Our Mutual Scarlet Boulevard** (1966–1970)

Map, where the year ends	41
For the honour of things, undone	43
The decision	44
Saffron Walden Blues, at the Pond House	45

Six Sonnets For Nathaniel Swift	48
Poem: 'to belong outside this catastrophe'	51
Six Street Songs	52

from **Flames on the Beach at Viareggio** (1970)

'England is bonny in May but small'	57
'underground carpark in the rain'	58
'the great and tragic bouquet of life'	58
Lost is the Day	59

12 Poems and a Letter (1971) (written with Elaine Randell)   63

Fools Gold (1972)   71

Dance Steps (For Paul) (1972)   79

Toad Church (1972)   85

Fog Eye (1973)

The Folded Man	99
Elegy	100
Love Song	101
Future Dream	102
Fog Eye	103

Pelt Feather Log (1974)   109

Starry Messenger (1975)   133

Black Torch (1978)

Prologue: Iron & Bread	139
Black Torch	141
Melrose to South Shields	163
Black Lamp Strike	167
Black Torch Sunrise	169

Uncollected Poems (1980–1990)

Jury Vet Told: Come Back & Learn the Way (1980)	177
Blood Money (1983)	184
Revulsion (1985)	188
Soft Hail (1988)	197
Ode: 'Completely Fragged in this New Dawn' (1990)	216

from Hellhound Memos (1993)

[5] 'Your tentship, your azureness, your cornflower'	219
[6] 'Sky so very vast and blue'	219
Hellhound Rapefield Memo	220
[12] 'So quiet tonight'	221
[14] 'Rachel, darkness'	222
Garbled Manifest – No Hellhole Unturned	223
[16] 'Jerusalem has been sold'	224
[17] 'The malevolent honeyblack'	225

from Postcards from Hitler (1998)

I am Lucifer	229
My Former Darling Country Wrong or Wrong	241

from Horses in Boiling Blood (1997–1999)

War Roses	247
Troubled Are These Times	249
Feast of Fashion Burning Down: Zone	254
Terrible Changes	261
Ode to Snowe	263
Victory Over Darkness & The Sunne	264
Cornflower	268
Cold Mountain Ode	270
Sam Arrives to Take Grandad for the Dawn Tickling	272
Memories Are Made of This	273
Love's Swanne Song	274
The Illegal 2CV	275
The Garden Door Is Open on the World	277

Forget About Her She Does Not Exist	279
At The Hoppings	281
I Don't Walk The Line All Of The Time	283
All of Your Sinnes Will Be Known Always and Never Forgiven	285
Petition to the Jesus Christ Almighty	286
Annie	287
Entrance to Heaven	288
The DollBird/Redblonde	289
Listen It's Plutting	292
Letter From Guillaume Apollinaire to Barry MacSweeney	294
Secret Poem Number Nine	295
1997	296
Rue Christine Lundi	298
Treasure	300
Lou's the Name on My Lips	303

Letters to Dewey (1999)   307

False Lapwing (2000)

False Lapwing	319
Pearl Standing Alone in Sparty Moonlight	321

Note on the Texts	322
Index of Titles	339

*In Memoriam Aidan McSweeney, 1992–2010,
and dedicated to Caitlyn McSweeney,
Barry's much-loved nephew and niece.*

Acknowledgements

The generosity of Paul McSweeney, for the Estate of Barry MacSweeney, has made this book possible. I am grateful for his good humour, encouragement, and enthusiasm. I am also grateful to Elaine Randell, for her permission to reprint '12 Poems and a Letter' and for a long conversation we had in 2013. I thank Jackie Litherland, also, for her comments on MacSweeney's late work. The librarians at the Robinson Library Special Collections, Newcastle University, and at King's College London Archives and Special Collections, have always been helpful. Special thanks to John Wells at Cambridge University Library for his help tracking down 'Pelt Feather Log'. I owe specific thanks to Allen Fisher, Ian Patterson, and J.H. Prynne for sharing typescripts and other materials with me over the years. Many, many other people answered my questions and queries, ranging from bibliographical arcana to personal anecdote and recollection. MacSweeney's work grew out of the collective life of independent presses and magazines, and I salute them all. Tony Frazer has overseen the present volume with patience and commitment.

'Toad Church' was published in *Chicago Review* in 2015, and I thank the editors Andrew Peart and Eric Powell for their sustained care with the text. The selection from *Horses in Boiling Blood* appears with the permission of Rod Mengham, for Equipage Press.

Lastly, my gratitude to Mark Roberts, whose enthusiasm for MacSweeney has been a source of surprise and delight to me for the past decade; and to Amy Tobin, always and entirely unfailing.

Introduction

Barry MacSweeney was an uncompromising and prolific poet. Between his first appearances in print in 1966 and his death in 2000, he authored two dozen books and pamphlets and published more than a hundred poems in little magazines. In his own archives at Newcastle University, and in the papers of his friends Eric Mottram (1924–95) and J.H. Prynne (1936–) there are many more unpublished poems and several complete sequences, some of which are represented here. Though there were periods where MacSweeney vanished from public view, his mental and physical health ravaged by alcoholism, the truth is that he wrote continuously. Yet like many of his contemporaries who emerged during the great poetry renaissance of the 1960s, he died with hardly any of his work in print.

In 2003, his selected poems—overseen by MacSweeney before his death and edited by Neil Astley—were published by Bloodaxe as *Wolf Tongue: Selected Poems, 1965–2000*. There's no question that this book contains some of his most important work: the serial poem *Brother Wolf*, which takes the life of Thomas Chatterton (1752–70) as a mysterious parable about poetic vocation; the obscure, anxious, and compressed music of *Odes*; the delirious and violent political satire *Jury Vet*; the plaintive and mythic *Ranter*; the late lyric masterpiece *Pearl*. But any selected poems is a compromise, and the story *Wolf Tongue* tells is partial and incomplete. While it captures the drama of the poet's life, it excises his genesis in the experimental poetry scenes of Newcastle, London, and Cambridge. The crucial period between 1966 and 1973, when MacSweeney first started to take poetry seriously, is represented by only six poems. His ambitious *Black Torch* (1978), highly prized by his peers, is left on the cutting-room floor. His final full-length sequence, the miraculous 'Letters to Dewey' (1999), shining with sincerity, appeared too late for inclusion.

These absences are understandable. MacSweeney's body of work is a complex one, propelled by internal logics of opposition: between harshness and sentimentality, confession and secrecy, avant-gardism and populism, collective life and individual struggle. He collected and abandoned his readers, often changing his style, making startling progressions from poem to poem and book to book. But as the present volume hopes to show, he never entirely gave up on the methods at his disposal. He was a critical reader of his own work, and as he progressed he also looked back to earlier phases of writing as a means of navigation. To borrow the terms of Raymond Williams, MacSweeney maintained a creative tension in his poetry between residual and emergent forms and styles. As the culture around him changed, he changed too, repurposing his work to meet the social demands of the day.

These unselected poems, then, should give the reader a deeper understanding of MacSweeney's achievement. It restores to view the volatility with which MacSweeney composed, read, and handled his poems. Beginning in 1968 with the publication of *The Boy From the Green Cabaret Tells of His Mother*, it follows the poet through political upheaval, personal disaster, and constant poetic vigilance. Drawing heavily on work published by independent presses, it testifies to the sheer commitment with which he and his friends attempted to change the literary landscape of British poetry. It's unlikely that there will ever be a true *Collected* MacSweeney, still less a *Complete*: he simply wrote too much, experimented too much, published too frantically too young. But perhaps this volume can work as a transitional signal, presenting new substance for future editions.

The Texts

The earliest texts printed here date from 1966, when MacSweeney was eighteen years old. Living in Newcastle he was surrounded by poetry. Tom and Connie Pickard's Morden Tower reading series brought American poets such as Allen Ginsberg and Gregory Corso to the city, and Jon Silkin's *Stand* magazine, relocated from Leeds in 1965, published an array of international poetry and comment. After leaving school, MacSweeney worked at the *Newcastle Evening Chronicle*, where he shared an office with Basil Bunting. Bunting, via his friendships with Ezra Pound and Louis Zukofsky and with his fierce loyalty to the North, offered the young poets an authentic modernist legitimation.

MacSweeney's first departure from Newcastle in 1967, when he was sent by the newspaper to study for a journalism diploma in Harlow, Essex, led to his debut standalone publication. The thirteen poems he wrote over the summer in Harlow were printed as *The Boy from the Green Cabaret Tells of His Mother* in September 1967. Privately circulated to the mailing list of *The English Intelligencer* magazine (edited by Andrew Crozier in Cambridge, with the assistance of J.H. Prynne, and later by Peter Riley), *Cabaret* was mimeographed on foolscap paper in an edition of 100 copies. MacSweeney re-used the title the following year for his paperback collection published by the major commercial firm Hutchinson. The story is infamous. Hutchinson, eager to capitalise on the beat explosion and the success of Penguin's *Mersey Sound* anthology, marketed the book and its poet aggressively. MacSweeney was nominated for the prestigious Chair of Oxford Professor of Poetry, and for a brief moment became a household name. He was reviewed, interviewed, and satirised in the broadsheet press, and gave many prominent readings. The book, which sold 11,000 copies, appeared in an American edition in 1969, featuring a dazzling psychedelic cover.

I have chosen to print the entirety of the 13-poem *Cabaret*, along with six other poems representative of MacSweeney's writing at the time. Though MacSweeney would later claim Hutchinson interfered with his manuscript, even editing the poems to remove expletives, there is no evidence to support this. But the status of *Cabaret*—existing as both a mimeo and a paperback, as well as a US hardcover—illustrates the difficulty and necessity of textual scholarship on the poetry of the 1960s and 1970s. The independent presses which MacSweeney favoured for the rest of his career were resourceful and inventive. Poems composed on the typewriter could be reproduced faithfully, inexpensively, and cheaply using mimeo stencils, while letterpress printing afforded the work a dedicated and exacting precision.

MacSweeney's next two books exemplify these two tendencies, with luxury and expediency existing side by side. *Flames on the Beach at Viareggio* appeared in 1970 from MacSweeney's own Blacksuede Boot Press in an edition of 150 copies. Vivienne Carlton, his then-girlfriend, selected the material from magazine publications and from manuscripts; his brother, Paul, provided the illustration for the cover. *Our Mutual Scarlet Boulevard* appeared in 1971 from Stuart and Deirdre Montgomery's Fulcrum Press, in both an elaborate subscriber's edition and a trade hardcover. Because *Boulevard* was delayed in going to press, I have re-ordered the poems by probable date of composition. The poems I have chosen from each book show MacSweeney extending the work of *Cabaret*, beginning to experiment with new forms. The later poems in *Boulevard*, 'Six Sonnets for Nathaniel Swift' and 'Six Street Songs' announce MacSweeney's discovery of disjuncture and seriality, pointing towards the next major phase of his writing.

After moving to London in 1970, MacSweeney began a relationship with the poet Elaine Randell, editor of *Amazing Grace* magazine. Their collaboration '12 Poems and a Letter' appeared alongside MacSweeney's *Just*

22 and I Don't Mind Dying as an issue of *The Curiously Strong*, published by Fred Buck, and later Ian Patterson, from Cambridge. Typical of the time, '12 Poems' was printed mimeo with one poem per page, surrounded by generous white space. It's impossible to reproduce the particular quality of attention and emotion that such presentation affords. The dimension of the page shapes the timing of reading: there's a music to it, which can only be gestured to here by indicating the page-breaks with a bullet point, thus: '•'.

MacSweeney's poetry developed rapidly during his relationship with Randell. Between 1971 and 1975 he wrote seven related sequences, starting with *Brother Wolf* and ending with *Starry Messenger*. This work has tended to be overshadowed by the *Odes*, collected in full in *Wolf Tongue*, where *Brother Wolf* also appears. Here, readers can see a different orientation at work. Following *Brother Wolf*, which MacSweeney worked on in notebooks for most of 1971, he produced *Fools Gold*—dedicated to Elaine—in a single sitting, on August 23rd 1972, publishing it with Blacksuede Boot soon after. *Dance Steps* followed next, written on November 22nd of the same year and printed the following month. There's something ceremonial about these texts, which combine a kind of stoned distraction with vivid meditative description. We see MacSweeney establishing and transgressing the boundaries of his poetics, learning and testing his moves.

By contrast, *Toad Church*, written between May and December 1972, while MacSweeney worked at the National Maritime Museum as a conservator of paintings, is a dizzying structure of fantasy and transcription. The poem was never published in full. MacSweeney was sensitive to criticism, and was easily dismayed if a poem received only lukewarm response from his interlocutors. It may simply be the case that MacSweeney was too busy to care if something fell through the cracks, always looking ahead to the next work. But the sequence *Pelt Feather Log*, published here in full for the first time, had a more protracted disappearance. Extracts were printed in Brian Marley's *Breakfast* and Martin Thom's *Turpin*, and the poem was scheduled for printing in 1975 by Tim Longville and John Riley's Grosseteste Press. But the press had trouble with funding, and by 1977 MacSweeney seemed to lose interest. There is no copy in his papers at Newcastle University, but the recently-accessioned treasure trove of J.H. Prynne's papers at Cambridge University Library holds three typescripts of the work-in-progress. The text here is based on what I believe to be the final version.

This raises the question of the limits of the present *Unselected* MacSweeney. There are clusters of short poems published around *Pelt Feather*

Log, printed in venues like the Eric Mottram-edited *Poetry Review*, and *The Human Handkerchief*, printed at the University of Essex. For the time being they must remain in the little magazines. I have emphasised MacSweeney's sequence-length experimentation, because this was the mode he favoured throughout the 1970s. As Bill Berkson wrote of Frank O'Hara's *Poems Retrieved*, the work represented here is 'refractive'. It throws new light on what we already know, and shows the poet in his mid-20s now gaining momentum, now halting and turning. The reader will find overlap and difference, gaps bridged by distortion, changed in echo.

The publication of *Fog Eye* was occasioned by the death by suicide of MacSweeney's friend, the poet Mark Hyatt. The book was letterpress-printed by Ted Kavanagh, with gorgeous pastel-pink wraps, in an edition of 200. Hyatt's work would appear posthumously with both Kavanagh (*Eleven Poems*, 1974) and through a Blacksuede Boot collaboration with Andrew Crozier's Ferry Press (*How Odd*, 1973). The final work in MacSweeney's cycle of serial poems, *Starry Messenger*, also billed itself as an elegy, this time for Galileo. It was first printed in the American magazine *Pod* (1976), edited by Kirby Malone, and was brought out as a chapbook by Elaine Randell's Secret Books in 1980, after the couple's separation.

While MacSweeney's appearances in American magazines were rare, extracts from his next major project *Black Torch*, first appeared in Fred Buck's *Bezoar* magazine, from Gloucester, Mass., in 1975. MacSweeney began the work while out on strike with the National Union of Journalists in December 1974/January 1975. While the bulk of the writing was complete by 1976, he continued to revise the sequence, researching the 1844 Durham Miners' Strike, and reading extensively in English labour history. *Black Torch* is one of the major missing parts of MacSweeney's work in print. It also presents his most sustained experiment with open-form composition, using the space of the page to maximum effect. The version of the book printed by Allen Fisher's New London Pride Editions in 1978 frequently uses the turning of the page for argumentative purposes. MacSweeney exploits the potential for sarcasm and irony in the embodied activity of reading. Like '12 Poems', page divisions here are represented by a bullet-point. I hope that the reader will find that the argument still rings out.

After Margaret Thatcher's Conservative Government was elected in 1979, MacSweeney's work became more viciously and despairingly political. The three offcuts from *Jury Vet* printed here marked the first appearance of MacSweeney's new style in print. Published by John Harvey's *Slow Dancer* magazine in 1980, these punk-inflected odes herald the nightmare of the

Thatcherite decade. They are violently problematic works. 'Blood Money' also appeared in *Slow Dancer*, and looks on with disgust at City Council politics in Newcastle. MacSweeney used the title again in the late 1990s for a sequence of sonnets, *Blood Money: The Marvellous Secret Sonnets of Mary Bell, Child-Killer*, which may yet still see the light of day. The previously unpublished poem 'Revulsion' is the last of MacSweeney's 'State of the Nation Bulletins', and joins those in *Wolf Tongue*: *Colonel B* (1979), *Liz Hard* (1982), and *Wild Knitting* (1983), as a convulsive register of disgust and dismay at English nationalism, unemployment, and rampant free-market capitalism.

The narrative provided by *Wolf Tongue* suggests that MacSweeney endured a long period of writer's block following *Ranter* (1985) and *Finnbar's Lament* (1986). But the papers at Newcastle University suggest otherwise. The moving long poem 'Soft Hail' (1988), previously unpublished, sustains the short-line of *Ranter*, swooping across the rural Northern landscape. It's true, however, that MacSweeney was unable to complete another long poem, titled 'No Mercy'. This exists in a heavily-annotated typescript, with much of the text scored out, and requires more textual archaeology than can be adequately represented in the present volume. A recording of MacSweeney reading the whole poem at Battersea Arts Centre in 1988 can be found online at the Archive of the Now.

MacSweeney returned to publishing in 1993 with *Hellhound Memos*, brought out by John Welch's The Many Press in a small chapbook. The eight poems here are those not included in *Wolf Tongue*: though this arrangement isn't entirely satisfactory, the reader can now piece together the whole sequence. The same year, his first selected poems *The Tempers of Hazard*, a joint effort with Chris Torrance and Thomas A. Clark, appeared from the commercial imprint Paladin. Like his foray with Hutchinson, the result has become notorious. Bought out by the Rupert Murdoch-owned HarperCollins, the poetry list was soon abolished and the volume swiftly remaindered and then pulped.

But with *Pearl*, published by Rod Mengham's Equipage in 1995, MacSweeney began to regain a larger audience for his poetry. *The Book of Demons*, which reprinted the entirety of *Pearl*, followed from Bloodaxe in 1997. This recognition coincided with the terminal crisis of MacSweeney's alcoholism. Though cared for extensively by his final partner, the poet S.J. (Jackie) Litherland, MacSweeney constantly relapsed into self-destructive drinking. While the lurid title sequence of *Postcards from Hitler* appeared in *Wolf Tongue*, the two long poems reprinted here show the fervent mixture of pessimism and bravado typical of MacSweeney's late work.

Litherland and MacSweeney visited Paris in 1997, staying near Père Lachaise cemetery and spending time with the American poet Stephen Rodefer, who in the 1990s split his time between Cambridge and France. This visit resulted in the last two sequences in this book. The 'collaboration' with Guillaume Apollinaire, *Horses in Boiling Blood*, was printed by Equipage in 2004. The 28 poems here make up two-thirds of the sequence, and consist both of the long expositions and brief lyrical apostrophes that delighted MacSweeney in the French poet's work. I have chosen not to include the complete book, because I want as far as possible to give equal weighting to each decade of MacSweeney's writing life. The sheer volume of poetry MacSweeney produced in the 1990s is overwhelming. He wrote frantically, often marking his manuscripts with whatever time in the dead of night he abandoned his work, exhausted. Such work can be exhausting for the reader, too, who tires of the performance, alert to its repetitions.

It is a special and poignant pleasure, then, to present MacSweeney's last long poem 'Letters to Dewey', which appeared in the Equipage pamphlet *Sweet Advocate* in 1999. Addressed to Rodefer's child, this work of steady emotion suggests a new opening at the close of MacSweeney's life. It is an advice poem, full of humour and regret, and begins to bring this volume to an end on a note of renewal. The final two poems, paired as *False Lapwing* by Peter Riley's Poetical Histories imprint after the poet's death, strike with hope and despair in equal measure. Printed on fine paper by letterpress, in the original edition they recall the care and consideration of the independent presses that supported MacSweeney, and that MacSweeney devoted his life to. It's my hope that *Desire Lines: Unselected Poems, 1966–2000* can do the same.

Luke Roberts

Further notes on the texts are located at the end of the book.

from

The Boy from the Green Cabaret Tells of His Mother

(1968)

The autobiography of Barry MacSweeney

Born in 'The Village', Benwell, Newcastle on Tyne, July 1948. Educated Rutherford Grammar School, best subjects art & english. About 1963 picked up in France a copy of Rimbaud's *Illuminations* and *The Drunken Boat*. Then Baudelaire, Laforgue. Wrote first poems at school. That was a sissy thing to do of course. Began job as reporter on local evening paper. Met Basil Bunting, poet. Met Tom Pickard and Jon Silkin. Showed Bunting *Walk* poem, it came back sliced down to about 4 lines and a note: Start again from there. My first real lesson. Reporting gave me a sense of what words could be: economy and just get down the *needed* things, with no frills. Open to the city and the country. You can walk out of Newcastle for half an hour and be in greenery. The city gave words a harshness, like the steel or coal. Then I wd flit off to little stone cottages on the fells and fish for trout, and pick mushrooms. & swim in the freshwater lakes. Began to translate Laforgue, Cros, Corbière.

1966–67: newspaper packed me off to Harlow Technical College, Essex, on a full-time journalist diploma course. An opposite life altogether. Synthetic new town, a dormitory to London. Its population, commuters with a vengeance. And the land was flat, that was a shock. An utter antithesis to Newcastle. Everything was so clean and clear-cut, and the people, they didn't *belong*, and had no roots in the town. Oasis. It was impossible to get involved. My eye, my colour/sluice became arbitrary for the first time. It was merely a funnel, and events and actions got a natural response from me. In Newcastle I was always too involved, always leaving pieces of myself against the walls. I wrote *The Boy from the Green Cabaret* poems in Harlow, and some political things for the first time. It was here I really woke up. Poems were fast and often, but it was bitter and solitary too. Spent days looking for some natural spot in the whole synthesis: found it, a small duck pond with sluice and lily-pads and footbridge. Told later it was one of the town planner's landscaping tricks.

Left here July 1967, *sans honneur*, carrying a bad character report in my hand & some poems, returned home to get the sack. But they didn't like the cut of my face either. Since then jobs as chief reporter in Cumberland, dole, reporter, social security, dole, gardener, dole. Now helps run Morden Tower poetry readings, and publishing posters and books. & of course writing poems. Wants to see poets get away from revisionism. Nobody returns in glory to Lucknow. and this is June, 1968, Newcastle.

To Lynn at Work Whose Surname I Don't Know

The sun always goes down
like this between the
staithes of the High Level Bridge,
dragging a golden plate across
the sewage,
          and then breaking it
among the rooftops of the
wharf-side houses and stores,
bending yellow slivers
up the mast of the red tug,
and on the starlings in the
chimney nests,
nooked in the lampblack and grey
shipping offices
          above Sandgate.

the dusty navvies
back across the Tyne,
sledgehammer at red-brick walls in the heat,
and slate eves, lugging
concrete heaps and half-bricks
with knotted hankies on their broad heads.

pedestrians this way down to
Mosley Street and back to work.

now i think i will come to you
and ask you and pour the Tyne
and the sun's bangles in your
lips and hair and bathe your
hands
in
this evening.

On the Gap Left After Leaving

1

When the coast
was not the coast
and sea was a shell
and shell-life was man,
    before the entire march began,
there had you, all you have now.
    before a crow
    flew across
    corn-mill flats
past the flat, hard elements.
before Sammy the poacher
ever tramped Killop
with half a dozen rabbits in the bag,
while all these houses
were fields and cowlands,
before the Paniards
were tractor-tooth bitten,
scarred with 1966.

2

In linctus eyes
that tell stories
of other stolen hours
the early harrow struck sun
reflects scenes
of dull ochre, squinting
through the gables of Tudor stone
in the orchard's heart.

3

Sun lemons
blaze in bubbles

(old means,
new, intricate designs), on leaves
    where in winter
i traced your hair,
when windows were sculpted marble white,
with frost, nightly—
    —frozen.

Walk

Tynemouth priory stands
sepia walled
hunched in bony remnants
of a holy rood,
gaunt anatomy of stones

cliffs plait
light brown and black
into shapes
        above the splash
        of paddlers

wind hoys sea

on shore,
        glassing to a sand edge.

Tynemouth curls like a cat
along the coast

the liner carries
the breaking of sky

sea is not for yielding
except willeks

& pale
crabs,
      sold on rough tables
      (hewn as roughly as the fishers)
these fishing towns, crofts,
the lighthouse, foyboats, foymen—

They are allowed.

How soon before
coalfish
haddock
cod
are cold as diamond
in quayside barrels,
before the hull strikes
waves again?
      again.
How long before
trawler crews rest their lids,
how long till nostrils are salt clean,
& fingers no longer grapple with nylon?

Then,
will they perch
like condors,
stooping for catches
with catgut claws?

It is not
of fish,
      the sea
         consists,

         it is not
      of water.

The Track, Fervour

each steel line fur to the wrist,
each man his own judgement,
to re-spirit the heart, churn the
vein roughly
to the platform of the muscles

it is a case of musicality and historical chance.
Kent in hazy june,
over the points,
        urgency in each nerve

look south look south
to the web about St Paul's
its scaffold crown
        hatching a blue sky
its engineers spidering the street

time is spared the honour
of rushing after.

   London air is clear, not sharp,
Compton St strippers
lack urgency they deserve,
cooly ask for sandwiches and beer

Rimbaud and Verlaine
swaggered in these same alleys
& the sun for Verlaine's rosary
after a lover's row

each friend away
from my outstretched hand,
and from my reason   oh
       tell me it is not so

Sealine

        woman lies on a couch of misery
            with her dreams.
oh fertile architecture that replenished my eye
    in dockland, where knotted groups
      of pickets shook me as a friend
& grabbed my shoulders bruising me even in
        their union strength. oh those cold lands i
   must cover before she will rest in peace
      on the shingle that clacks on the hulls
    of Cuban sugar ships,

          the weak brine of the thames as oily
    it oodles round the wharfs. those delicate pebbles
and shells and waves those masts and store rooms
    those cruel times by
        the sea's foundation

Bladder Wrack Blues

the sea is pregnant with bladder wrack
    your bed was a groaning ship sounding
        out the ocean floor

your house was a box where i kept my shoes
    your chairs were bright blue & electric
        but that was yesterday that was tomorrow
      & never today

A Letter, This Far Away, Tonight for Liberty

1.

walking to post the other letter
its form exact in my pocket & the sun
behind chimneys
& round the corner it splashes on the
trunk of a single oak,
     trickles through fences
     dappled in tiny ivy diamonds.

2.

a pine cone
rolls towards me
turns upside down
and stands in my palm with the
chunky stance of a screech owl

slits under its mail
give it the effect & carriage
of a Samurai—
  a pine cone rolling
  at the feet of every man,
  sodden with many trampled streets,
  never inquired after.
so Benno Ohnesorg, I dream of the spirit
and fracture of the one-month-old sacrament.

I stand alone in the Krummen Strasse,
whirlpools and windmills ahead of my feet.

the apex of the spirit and flesh dont stand
a chance in the arms of Moloch.

a cone rolls across Europe from this tree
where I stand beneath the sun, sets over
west Berlin,

a white mark on the curb,
a red mark on the spare ground,
the oak tree a fabulous truncheon
the black acorns are thunderclouds over Europe

One Year Old, The Wilted Hybrid

    in this town bushes are a second warmth.
       in this town everyday there is no
  friendship
            & a blanket
    of events curtails us:
     seeing the galaxy as a red
truth cast on poor soil
  on a poor root of person
       who all belong somewhere else yes
    they all belong elsewhere.

  the flower-delicate mind is a
     replete dormitory
 shaped against actual climax
     or climatic sweat, a gin distillery
is the heaviest industrial concern,
      and that phrase photographs the replete
          heads,
                companionship we lack

& The Biggest Bridge is Forty Feet Long

        a dream so far in me as to be in my
very arteries. quilts of rain lashing into
          peat, a light-handed wind picking
      drops off juniper clumps.
      ruinous action and other friends
inside these houses   ,
                     as if hydrogen
    were the entire possibility
into spaces, this town sleeps day in
     night outside is broken
  by loudspeakers, speak-easy is the
tongue of this town, the alfalfa, chlorophyll
       shining under the canopies
   in the precincts.

    ii

   cobbles tramlines & winkle packets
      budgie eggs in sawdust, shredded tobacco
in a faltering hand, an unerring man. steamy
      nosed children of this city,
   dazzling dark. it could be 1926 another fantasy.
     the children of this town are
          not of this town, principally.

On the Burning Down of the Salvation Army Men's Palace, Dog Bank, Newcastle

They stood smoking damp and salvaged
cigarettes mourning their lost bundles
each man tagged OF NO FIXED ABODE.

Mattresses dried in the early sunshine
blankets hung over railings and gravestones
water and ashes floated across the cobbled hill.

A tinker who wouldn't give his name
bemoaned his spanner, scissors and knife-grinder,
which lay under 30 tons of debris.

Water on the steps in the dining room
but none to make a cup of tea

Tangled pallet frames smoked still,
men lounged around mostly in ill-fitting
borrowed clothes others naked in only
        a blanket or soaked mac.

We looked at the scorched wood and remarked
how much it resembled a burnt body later we
heard it was charred corpse
we remarked how much it resembled burnt-out timber

The Axe

as an instrument
& means of persuasion
lacks elegance:

its affections are
over-lustful, its
attentions are soon ended,
its face too polished,
too chic & its look
is criminal

but the tongue
with its silver
bushels of dainty
                lightning,
cracks the woodblock
of evil down the centre,

showing the grain.
here we find the poet
stamping out fires made
by the wood-shavings from
other mens heads.

The Boy from the Green Cabaret Tells of His Mother

Lady powders the nourishing teat
in her platform of bricks.

Vapour, azure smoke, ash
drifts over the gravel-pit.
A blond boy gossips with carp & tench.
His mother, draped black, traipses mountains
for her sergeant-at-arms.

A grizzly kiss is Liberty.
A drunken hug is worth a revolution.
Trumpets blast! Bugles wallop out a reveille!
—it is an urchin wiping her nose on rags—

My sleeping-bag is the Plough, slicing
cloud-pillows, nightcaps from moonrays!

Rain, cheap beer—
White thunder on my collar—
A boot next to my heart—
kicking over bowers & stadiums—
Fabulous underground rivers of foxgloves—

The mail-coach upturned,
wheels spin like planets,
poems pinned to its shafts!
Dames, merchant, musketeer,
in the dead season.

They lodge in a liver-coloured
slab-drab morgue, eyes shooting out
red as radishes! Flesh tinted
with the gradual shellac of Death.

The Poet scrawls his testament—
his ink freezes, jelly mixture of soot
and red wine. His ranks are deplete,
the chains of his body jingle.

Grapeshot tatters canvas, cold is
bone-deep; the black widow flounders,
the river sucks out her unbroken maidenhead;
she screams wildly–Delight!
The blond boy knots his handkerchief,
tears up newspapers, picks louse off his neck.

He turns over sees a glass of electric violets.

The Copper Heart

prisoners & brides tear at geraniums
its copper wings in the bars of their heads

marine chariots of pearl and tungsten
poems drizzling from fat volumes

tulips drip blood gouts
children pick sunshine adults burn bread

lets tear down forests drink the sea
dry take off every stitch of clothing sprawl   in the corn
    madness

City

Workers go home whatever wherever
Lynched with expensive pleasure
Pockets heavy with paper the hour when
City jams in the lights red amber green
Blood copper-coin leaves

Pebbles rattle beneath their black boots!
Shrouds draw across the network!
Closed doors hide corrupt perfume
Rising from carcasses in parliamentary abattoirs

Love shrivels like plastic in an iceblue gas flame
A dark shrawl hangs over us

Pain is tolerant this the hour when any
Reasonable thing sleeps hugging a
Bruised side sullen with waiting

Song

cast me back to
the ferry and foy
to late december
        snowy hills
between the Allen and Tyne

oh back back
        to sheep's shag back
to Dog Leap Stairs
where burns
the groin
        of my intent

Pastoral

Soft, soft bark in water,
fresh as cress.

The blue cattle of your eyes
grazing on the green of mine.

2nd Telephone Song

Emeralds, spa-rock chips
quartz slivers if all these
fell on this same stretch
of black straight path &
rickety hedge none cd
compare with the
cracked gaunt slip of finger
nail pointing as
some bright star thru
years and years & joy
along which we sailed
in eyes of storms in
sunshine & rain
(yr bright fingernail
brings yr voice past
terraced wardrobes a
grocery store the motor
way to this humble bright
& oh so willing nest
of outward going concern
for you for you for you

The Decision, Finally (for Jeremy Prynne)
4 a.m., March 24 Sparty Lea

And we have the decision,
which was ready made,
      and now its clear
      and, as they say, cleared up.
What have we to fight for,
save books, and contours,
and the tidal bore,
and the way we behave?

we have the decision
without bitterness, with
a *resignation*
to the facts which are *these:*

      there is a land, a people,
      among ourselves, too, for
      this is a legacy, already
      said,
          the golden legacy,
      to beat into coin.

I am a minter of coins.
Let's not forget that.

To Me Mam, Somewhere to the North of This Shit

1

Even dark North Sea fish are
caught in the net of the absentee landlord
whose province is not land but total
possession of the soul
        (butterflies & princesses
lie deflowered in the snow) I mutter a cold prayer

2

Women stem their blood flow for love &
cry about their children at night in
the lonely lovers bed
which I taste & you taste & we all taste
which is beyond the holiness of their
position & possessions   me mam is a
stooping figure shovelling coal from
the path into the cellar & she
worries, not like a hound worrying a rat, but
       like a star worries
    the ocean,
who fears no reflection

from

Our Mutual Scarlet Boulevard

(1966-70)

Map, where the year ends

Allendale,
        north beck
        plays pastiche at main stream,
twirl trout in shallows.

Sparty Lea Cemetery
lies by the Allen,
        willows cleared
        shallows dragged,
fish take night for home.
poplars wave above farmers' bones
        'and their beloved son Dixon
        died Oct 26 1916
        aged 11 months'…

Year's end village celebration.
    brass band, bonfire.
men in shot silk—red, primrose, turquoise—
    faces blackened with burnt cork,
    ritual disguise.
15 to midnight,
    the wending to the square, gloved.
    men of the village march
disguised in clown's nose,
actor's lip and eye, like kiddies' soldiers,
carrying barrels
blazing with woodchips soaked in tar.

        publisher, poets, wife & son
        return to fell cottage;
        raw whisky, cider,
        slab-cold wine.

Dawn.
poet couched in bracken
in dale where sheep find shelter

gun cocked under coat.
cat's eyeing pheasant, partridge,
    Lord's Bailiff
with warrant for arrest.

pâté on toast, burnt kettle
cocked on fire range.

Allenheads.

here river disappears
through mineshaft
under fell.
out at Dovepool,
    where Sam the Poacher
    woke to find his 27 pigeons
marble-winged
storm-eyed
necks bitten & sliced through by whippet's jaw.

sips bitter above the stream,
tweed cap, greatcoat stripped of buttons
(age, not ignominy)

gaffs trout on Lord Allendale's land.

For the honour of things, undone

the ravel is in the eye
the foot's putting down

from Essex out,
        300 miles
         by diesel
through Yorkshire to home.

feeling numb is easy here
on my pawing ground.
these things undone
i can say i'm sorry.
        but what purchase is that
        to you with so much love.
again, remember the tongue-less bells.

    the spring is cold
    and clear,
            March drizzle
    on my brow
    says sorry
    for the sun's paling.

The decision

twig cuts
        moon
in three,
        brightly on the
        village square,
        stream's going down
        crosses the night,

        through tunnels.

the moon brilliant
a pear in a basket,
an image for now, for the
feeling I have here.

I have never felt so alone,
so unattached to those near
me, this has no place, no
specific heat to it,
        a moment,
gone, and the gaslight in
your eyes, new eyes,
old ones renewed,
their pleasure.

Love may grow from this
circumstance, then I'll
shake your hands.

Saffron Walden Blues, at the Pond House
for Jeremy Prynne

1

I read the
rain on the turf
feel it, sitting on this low barrel,
despite a thick
scarf. the roads are winding he said,
and my feet go on, one follows the other,
each time.

2

my means to some are dubious. the
law which herds men up who herd
together is inverted protection.
blue groups, against
shopkeepers, unions (any sort), bankers, road
menders, innkeepers

>they search for a happiness that doesn't hold
>water anywhere, feel unwanted, more like
>un-needed, rightly so

I imagine Villon
riding through this village
a posse of *flics* at his back
not standing any chance

3

>I sit at this desk, smooth wood under my palms,
>rub it,

feel grateful & gentle toward you, you whose house
this is: like Lindisfarne, I knock, and the grey habit
keeps the seas and police away; my horse tires
and needs shoes

    & that implicit trust, welds
    a certain emotion down, keeping
    it right

        keeping myself right is
        hardest

4

        ivy around his latch
        is any man's dream. i
am no Anarchist, or Antichrist
but a dreamer running at will.

& the farmer crops ivy with an axe
for choking the stone and strangling
any growths;
        so there is the full
        parable of ivy in the air,
        & the households of men
        are inhabited by lice
        (singers, book salesmen),
& their goods rot. this is good, a
necessary part of the dream.

i latch onto ivy easily.
& here, surrounded by quiet music,
mozart, ravel; maps,
stone.

i think of times gone,
when we sat on cold benches.
cold hours, days they were
at the fount of cities. Love
is no means dead, and this story
is a bastard born, fatherless.

i am father to nothing,
especially that which bears my blood, my name.

i belong and am exiled.
exile is not a state of thinking,
but thrown into strange places, unwillingly.
i come from the Chillingham Bull.
i have no latch, not even ivy
to choke mason's work.

but more venom than an adder.
more
    eyes than sand,
and a soul that rings like brass.

Six Sonnets for Nathaniel Swift

1

When leaves fall   it tastes sweeter
Than ever. Colours smoothe out in the casino; a man's
Another empty shard (not red like Gary's gift); blue
Green rustle   see how the equalising spinning
Traces across the face of love

Click. His poker face snaps

Her mouth is beautiful stealing my letter B
Lethally a truss tightens   we look for a frantic
Evening to lift us out of another boring afternoon
Do you think your breath will escape   gamble on
Such meagre chances   pushing out warily
from the sable mouths of the inert hill-climbers
Stripping off before thee, blind
Whispering for the perpetual Yes.

2

Recognisable demons approach speedily on their machines
Simmering with intentions. Is my face an intention any
More than your suits which are chic foliage
Stolen from Dunsinane.   the demons go backwards
I think I'd hide my leaves along the eastern coast
Fred is writing poems mentioning the pollock fish
The sand smoothes out his sinus. When we
Possess everything like now   even what we haven't at hand
Trying to shield all bent days (thanks Jack) turned proposals
Milk pedestals where we enjoyed being young
If it rains the cat will come indoors   or borrow your umbrella
An educated animal; please watch out for yourself
It is an easy index to Read   that Abel hands over
You could learn to Write it out in hours,   not days

3

Chester Expletive limps with his errand; he
Tells of a man in black. Sleuth of Molly's pegnoir
His star receded like any true faun.   Spurs
Found stairs & open door.

Father, Madre Mia, grace this tin breast with oily eyes
Anoint this stubble with sweet unsullied hands

I don't believe you can be 'sullied' by anything

Drunk, impatient with his bad 'swim', the priest
Led him away to a step in the chancel   fed him
Under-cooked bacon piped him the rainbow end of
Anguish.   O Mother smote this lip from your hem

Starry eyed sleuth swimming on his oily tin lip
Impatient with the rainbow on the stairs and stubble
Being transfused with 'fast-milk'.

4

Id-less Uniform extends *its* hand to keep the
Silver ball roulant; we produce a faltering spunkiness
This is the end of August 1969   a Thursday which
Is cracker-barrel, no?   The reed dampens
In my soprano saxophone *Meditations* though
I'm not in a hurry. Will it rain falling upon
The pointless cherubs ('the sweet pretty things'); silver
Hands roll the mind down slopes to the station, a
Cracking Thursday as the reeds murmur pointlessly, 'un-
-Ecstatic'. We now know from one end of this town
To the other, that *its* hand isn't *its* own, silver
Wrists and rolling eyes snatching for the sweet pretty
Thursdays, meditating   the soprano cherubs, The Hand
Each day goes out to chamois the dingy purlieu.

5

'The Forbidden Pictures.' Nude passer-by
Notices an old man and young woman holding a grave
Conversation on the promenade, at the theatre,
Dressing-room, stage, a red dancer indicts a grotesque couple;
Emil's labour;   I mean, *Ungemalte Bilder.* 1938-45

I think I may have what you describe as 'profane eyes'
And the poem that sometimes falters,

'A bold dip into the dustbin
Of the ages
Can sometimes produce astounding illumination'
Oh
I wonder if i sign these squibs to avoid pressure
Or invite with my campari

Scanning for mexican lyrics; 'two sorrow-laden crochets'

6

I never see a whippet but I think of the ideals of
American patriotic freedom. Havoc
Pours into the room around us   a submarine
With a faulty blow-hole; shadows on our hands
Remind us immediately of de Chirico's painting
Of the pigtailed girl bowling a hoop...

The radio moans for its teething ring

Sufferings make the seasons wild
Shadows draw closer to the stone.
Three years   long days   a moth
Skirts the light
Trace of its shadow;   shadow & light,
The reasons in the half-light
Move us again   towards.

Poem

to belong outside of this catastrophe
and not permanently receive
what charitable boxes are carried down-valley
to this solitary
farm ... where the oak thrives
through all seasons with human water
dropped from
only inward eyes....
                         another night
and I again lose my knot in the
inextricable passé that recklessness brings—the
china walls break easily enough, stop there

'no City, nor Cornfield, nor Orchard: all is
Rock & Sand;'

the dead weight (and loss) of past infamies
keels over any real desire; (is it desire, or a lunar wish
to avoid another contract
in the public cornea
where I always topple into the falls
and Bruno saves *me*! to-
-day the courtyard is slack, an eye
behind those compartmented deceits
might ease one mistake; but
passion and reluctance, after
hurried apologies, these, like
so much rain   move as the day
does   we call it 'weather', draw isobars
through intricate pardon.

Six Street Songs

the heart is in the
brothel. but only in
dream. defenceless as salt, we
coach along. he comes
to my door, but
i know no magistrates. only
by reference to death. the
heart is in
the brothel's door, or
the street.   the kinetic
motor cycle crashes
through your dream bag.

You are breaking my arm. the
      one of angry frustration, a
      bottle rack in my throat. john
clare's hoe ripping through
the blind.   one hand on the bell
      t'other handcuffed, my ghost
raps
where i cannot knock. no use at all.
no one needs you.   foreign,
uncut pages.

life just seems packed with
critical youngsters, and
my joy, pre-raphaelite kisses. the
     music is where we are, loud
and pointless.   Verlaine grumbling
about youth through the foggy cordite; his
arch cowboys and wrecked matelots. my
lusty asteroids whirl in with
a burr, the cowboys take to the sea, i
don't know how i got here;   another
grubby plimsole catches me
     dazzled by the sun;   though
     the tree-line
     at the terminus
is kinder.

I wonder if your trans l'Europe express
has arrived in Antibes; will you
drink a little brine for me there. I've
     lost the need
     for your tambourine, this
     time I think it will last.   I just
can't afford you; your hunger, or
your fading presence.   the loud
rock and roll won't cover
it up.   you've swayed about long
enough. thousands of styles
     but not one poem. brine
and the tambourine
floating out along the sandbar. no
poems.

Where is her head lying
as in the vast aeroplane of night
I float by with opiates.
    at the sunny terminus
    the rails
just shoot off into trees.   Verlaine
grumbling about youth
    through the foggy cordite. I don't
know her, I call her Bonney.
    on the canvas, I'm far left,
don't move, though
    the tree-line
    at the funeral
is blinder.

rags flapping in the branches. mockery
flung back as snow. you
    make me wait outside
like a page-boy
in a myth about the Holy Grail. I
love you in your
present state. Mallarmé writing a poem
    at his son's death-bed. where
    is the shadow, how
    you might need
    destruction
of my heart's peace. I have
talked to the servants,
but it is too late.

from

Flames on the Beach at Viareggio

(1970)

Poem

1
England is bonny in May but small
& like a faded outlaw I tell you there isn't enough room
but you never go.

2
I sit beneath the freshly blooming lilacs and read "Two Pieces"
by O'Hara, I could have said Frank, but I'm not fond of operetta;
I'm fond of you, stretching beneath the fronds, fondling
My awkwardness;   I run over you like a green truck
with golden stars painted on the bonnet. You're in love.
You never leave. When you do, it's never spring, & I'm
inextricably tangled in the doomy january evenings
listening to something moderne, feeling your absence
cover me like a shawl so I am eventually totally blacked out
as if I was at war with someone: I am only "at war" with
the thriving syndications of this city, London. I'm in love.
I admire Léger's brassy men. You fondle my fondness once too
often & we end up sleeping among the pronouns like fresh young
verbs at their first sentence.

3
a Boeing passes, momentarily drowning the jazz; rain.
it is such a relief not to have to listen to him breathing,
or dwelling on his fragmented life, an insect
as he is, a cockroach, beetling beneath the stars,
lost in recordings of other's creations.
settling between the toes, he licks his nib, & writes.

4
lost in a trance of parity, I can't go. pills don't help,
they make me wary of meat. i half-heartedly chew the kidney
i once did so deeply need. no amount of Air France flights
could carry this. your attractive frayed hem. may the modal
english green deepen to scarlet as the sun sets why not.

Poem

underground car parks in the rain. mockery
      flung back as snow.

Bysshe, you
would love this rain ;

flames on the beach at Viareggio.
      not only flesh burning.

the whole of English poetry too. no
amount of snowballs
can douse it.   any
number of hearts.

Poem

"the great & tragic bouquet of life".

I couldn't have written that.   amber fumes
float through the approaching hands, though.

You can't read the penguin book of permissive society
all your mingy days.

    1959 was too early for all of us.
nowadays the line has to be longer.

the line in the poem has to be longer than in 1959.

Poem

Lost is the day.
No soaring.

Each ascent I make, nightly, is
refusal, angers
land-locked captains.

There is a roaring in my head never stops.
I lie beside you, touched
by your tiredness; I hardly ever sleep.

Floating around the meniscus
on a raft of weeds.
                          On whose secret shore
Adam is jubilant for fruit.

November 5 1970

Twelve Poems and a Letter

(with Elaine Randell)

(1971)

Well now,

                I am at work
        my boss comes back
   hastily   into oblivion

The letter
my desk

•

Well
down
electric

The letter was
       35
  —think about
         clinging

•

in you too"

           people moving
Had to stop there. Call
      on a blue fjord.   so

   touched
In Amsterdam I listened
     in London i

Was discovered

•

                It is
my dear old mum
        every weekend.   I'm going
on Sunday

          singing sweetly

    I can see all the people moving

•

              This afternoon I feel
                  her in the National

            Beckenham tonight
        coming over
him

    before
Did I tell you

•

          I've

tried
Did I tell you

          saying

              as the boat

left

        "I wonder if those concrete
     in the rain
   a loud and wonderful voice

           of the Gods"

•

a sheep
of the Hook.   if I lived
Enclosed
     because you drink

   I wonder.

       maybe

someone
out as Barny
     I really have to eat.

•

   I must tell
   someone

Right, now I really have

       it's strange

"I run my hand"

    I've always loved
        I feel I should
      maybe not—perhaps I'll
    have guessed
    what you know

we'll have to
        forget

•

        we'll spend some crazy night in a real
  Monday
   but it isn't so I
fright
Away to Beckenham and back

•

    back to try on
  angels   over
Barnet tonight

some poems

•

  Can I look
outside
    the sanity

I get
A small bird

In winter snow
     on the trees

•

We
slot
your voice
    my dog

moves
   the salt

We leave

Fools Gold

(1972)

for Elaine

Sip marrow, the arm is
turned blue towards
the land, through a funnel
of double-time.   He
uses both eyes, the com-
passionate table is empty
now.   Moon is a planet
through a geographer's
lens. The last and first
time, the music is soft.

Inhabit a bottle of
milk and sail away: you
wash I'll dry, all of
that.   The violin, the
millennial harsh trombone.
An easy glutted mark.   Be
ware, let the pan wander.

The dream is quenched
loosestrife in his making
fingers: free of swimmer's
grease, he will sink in
abeyance for gold.   The
helicopter on the beach
is quite saurian, rest
in the syphon of green.

Reverse your track down
the funnel:
          tiny sparklets
of optimism along the sea-
gas pipes, can a reliable
plumber be found?   Worn
away with staring at Venus,
he licks his fat, the slumber
of basil.

See your spiked shoes
are by the wall, run
with the tide.
            Pyrites
on the staircase of Job,
bracken ankles in his
digital pie.   Come with
me: the moon is bright
and we are alone again.

All the women look
Hungarian, they trudge
out of triangular postage
stamps, they wear melon
rind. Their gypsy dogs
wag & bark on the estuary
shore;   climb back, throw
your rucksack in the salty
gutter.
       Her tea is bright
red, time has no reward
and the marriage is broken.

Aberglaube and flaked ore
rinsed with coots' blood.
In the rich family of timeless
hunger, he
      proposed her name
Galena, he looked inside
the sheltered porch;   clouds
scorched his ears. Only moss
grows in the cracks.

Put my hand in
yours: it is quite
French with tacks
in the palm.   Others
see the sky as an ecto-
lunch, a final duff
of hope.
      Name any neon
scallop shell, scrips
of veined marblings.
Leave the harbour now.

Find this while aim-
lessly scuffing other people's
shoes to self-destruct
five seconds from now.
                No
fate like the handy
present you give
me is so pale and quiet.

There is a wasp beneath
his wild beret, cheroots
in his frenzied mouth
resemble fingers.   He
flicks them off up
to the elbow how
can he know?   All
for fevered pauses
to call for this with-
in your touching normal hair.

Bathe in scum then, spread
feint talcum over
the world. Kestrels
make good houseguests
at every turn, claws
are the true symbol
of any bilious neo
platonic gambler.   Salt
is a hurricane, who
can you be with now.

You have a licence, you
may travel anywhere with
brief motion.   We can
exchange spherical names
of gold.   In arm
or neck the lowly
suns obey.   Lie on a shelf
all summer, swipe flies
with slender wands of
galena spa.   He is ill-
iterate and thoroughly tanned.
The tide follows him by.

Draw the napkin
down, extract the
inner secret worm.
How so much better
to feel like this
you say, I'm burning.
Clamber on the vestal
railway, you will
compare your filthy
sheet with any false
apache, so touched
with fire he dies.

Make dawn amalgam
with the fastest
of rare metals, for
you will sign the
very crust away.   Thus
a psittacosis floods
your fevered pores,
that's a shag of fire.
The garnet in his hair
so royal with light.

Written at Lade Halt,
Romney Marsh, Kent
on August 23rd 1972

Dance Steps: For Paul

(1972)

tagore's snakes & flowers
pre-raphaelite toothpicks
in your shop window
i don't know how you meet the demand
but you do

*

in a book on the cosmology
of furtherance
you place goethe
next to werther
in a small shed
in the rain
you will go far
& it will cost you nothing

*

i throw my knife down
cynical again
you scold and
make me blush
because fortresses
with holes in the side
are useless to everyone
the potatoes get peeled

*

you walk with her
back through dante's nostrils
into rosetti's gasflame
of bright continuances
say, you say, how do
you keep your floor
so clean
and all that shit
in your head

*

the heart is weak
it's no good to play football
with
but the lungs
make excellent goalposts
they let the rain through
you pick my teeth
with a vulture's claw
so good to know
such good friends

*

the feedback
of memory
stalks down
my shoe
up into my chest
and out my head
via the mouth
"piper at the gates of dawn"
moves from one channel
to another
i have my stethoscope
and now i'm walking away

*

you sent me a cloud
which was very english
of you
as if you knew
john betjeman
of backgammon fame
the sky-like mackerel
but slit open
guts in a barrel of salt
rub it in it hurts

*

i try not to be cynical
moody or flippant
but when you have two legs
like everyone else
and you feel different
it makes life very difficult
and square

*

we revolve
all parts of the cyclical
revolution in space
our heads turn
then our feet
until we are quite
dizzy
in the next century, suddenly

*

non-toxic to protoplasm
a perfectly biochemically
balanced and harmless
compound salt
this is an accurate
piece of information
before lunch

*

none of your shoddy
tricks here
he said
put your hair
where your mouth is
and suck

*

"making love
is like a long poem"
what a haiku!

*

by the river
eating snow
for breakfast
soaking wet
what a long winter
i photograph myself
bleeding
then tear it up
for fun

*

light
in the sky
travels through
my head
here you are
some for you

November 20th 1972

Toad Church

(1972)

1.

You're not wheat you're puke on a stick. Air, a
way of nothing, church of th'emeraldine toad.
Tongue in the exit, care for
   the correspondence of angels. They went
 before.
o Wild Wheat blowing, churning the blue and shadeless
o spikelet of cinnabar
bend like a tree, wave like a man of barley

the tapping is a clown's nose
   the wild elastic, snapped and brown

Antlers of the pale envelope
           sealed until dark

with the music of the stolen forest-radio.

2.

   steam of the metal cylinder & gin.
      the Bead is a light in his ear, how
   can he hear.
Wild Heather Clover various supple Barks
made listless illusion
   in the charm of his Antlers.

   Tuft woven in a scream of the beach-radio
held him as a rainbow
   in a more expansive pill

Swelling, mutant grotesque!   Know your sudden book
   well.

3.

   this isn't relief from prayer this is the Toad Church.
     Relief from lust in a cool pouch of fennel-seed.

    o dim light reddened by electric pre-eminence
    o bath-water run by heaven and drained outwards
   With a timely grip on the anatomy lesson

   Sky Commodore, brief me with solitude
   & accuracy of eye, those small green squares below

     amyl nitrate mouthwash, the telephone says more.

4.

O white virago, Doll of ether, air streaked
  with madder upon black, upon
the grey ghost of someone else's muscle & bone

    Nor may they move from that awful honeyed light

Fold my belt with a woman, will she be straw
  with raw gold and thunder
Does light make sense of sound in the ear
o lustful patois
  iron, excess alcohol and light

5.

   We, for blue & green, seen mistakenly as tearing
after pieces
   Padded slink for my feathered car, in his brain
of icy particles & sand
     Smoke surrounds his water-bead

   Whose book of model aeroplane glue
   Whose unbending orange bed
   Whose bland faceless passion

In a storm of plucks, the tongue turns words into an
   O.

6.

   of a more or less Expanding bead they spoke.
Temple of the excursionist their overdrive and light.

   spiky yellow buds between his making fingers
midnight charabanc of nerve-ends lacing
     you are briefed with aberglaube and flaked ore

o Abandonees of minus-a-third, your mint wreathed
    his illusory antlers spelling death
Mordent enthusiasm, your touching normal hair

7.

    Snap me.
      Lower your eyes I am your father coming home.
       Valve these illusory callipers with otherwise
metaphorical distress, you the yellow-hammer
      in my iris' bed.
Always pump towards the open oceans, bend
   with pasture, lean upon a wheel
of fortune and Be
damned the loathsome rest.   Eyes
   remain,
    and Winkles treat us vastly.

8.

  with soft hand-pressure you anneal smoke.
Toad
    with an immense parade of cellular spawn
      anomorphosises the futuristic emerald church. Green
as the river
   green.
Disregard, the hell of all unlooking. One
fatal parade, in a wrath of oscillation.
  Silver as the hoof of the moon,
chancel specula, cope of gems called Beryl.

9.

He is excited because a bun flies by.   Those
people will just throw anything, on mono
  phonic bursts.
  Count me, out of the sudden way.
He cannot kick the ball because he is inside it!
(the stars fall back on the beach & are absorbed).   The
    rest is skin.
Call me whore, the shoes of any citizen in NW 8.

10.

      white enamel blinds
each of my efforts in this hot kitchen of souls
an ardour of pure breathlessness
  you bring me
(Thulean pessimism enters yr senses via/
  yr nietzschian eyes

   Play chess, beneath wild canopies of pests, the
crass normalcy
of his hands
 in the hand
 of whatever you sat to a toad
after Beryl's crystal crumbs

11.

   Toad is an insect phenomena of the age / wax
meridian I whistle within tawny bubbles
     as would the scarlet cameleopard rise
     against the phoenix Ozymandias
     (yr dream of ants writhing on a sill
        your mouth is painted turquoise
      or it isn't painted at all
      quite blank
     I love you equally (but
      separate colours)   all rancid
with beer rivets and brown flies

12.

       mastoids before a bust
   of Nelson, Nancy
   the joy in the museum of your nostalgic
     leg-iron
 the first binoculars in the world, the first clocks
o Carmichael whales like an image of mad taps
o groundbase & mercurial cinnabar in an Everett
And the world only takes form outside of the car
    trunks trees & brass plates spinning in the wind

13.

     Room's gold threatened madder
    peristaltics you swooned.   The snow
   burst suddenly!   Sung under pink
universal sequins coating the divine
     Bing Crosby. Hoopla! Snowshoes! Purple
stag-spiders in the birtwhistle hour! (by the
   pool destrung instruments at dawn / isn't
that obviously green, like toad, and the fire
 in his green gut we dream. Of her. Of
both green pairs of lips, burning.   Or come
split in ice-toed pine flecks on Valerie's bones!
    Through an opium funnel, arm turned blue towards table
      so soft I pushed the blazing bread-knife through.

14.

  Toad hangs illuminated fetters on my door. His
nostalgia burns with hiring blood & lowly greed
across front-page loathings.
Her face her mountain hair stream
    with handcuffs and chains.   Pockets are empty
   he chuffs a silver-still me.   Your hands
are pleated bands of colour contrast and shape
in the self-propelling pirate grind
(those gloucester hills are one in ten)
   I will eat the placenta of the future
church,
    flicker/ on/ off/ in the daylong night & dome
of love.

15.

   He faints in a sweet field of orache & purslane.
   Behind his blue yearning looks madder upon blackgold
writhings, whose burning rusty apocalyptic sword invades
   your loin-law.   Nouveau Crap at the rudder
in the latchwork house of glands, adrift & toxic
puny gestalt prince.

  Piss like that, gush spiky yellow contrition
up the wall
  You south & tartan smock sheath (my Guinevere)
the purple loosestrife in your mountain hair

 Vodka, flung into the mummer's face
the neoplatonic way you're no gambler any more.

& drive me home (mad drunk with mimicry) alone.

16.

Cards and dice in my eyes for you across the rough
wooden table as the cribbage board folds have the
shadows of some former mystery diluted from speaking
in too many different tongues that no one understood.

17.

     (In the shade of Horbiger & Leviticus
  the antlered dream their sullen forest-radio with soul-
     butter we're sliding out of the room on)

when sand drugs my loom my wheelbarrow my purpose, hurled
and wrapped incisors trumpet forever theocracry, strongest
oaks glimpse trembling at the sacred planet's hymning
death in factories schools and shops, slashed with grey
tedium

18.

    sheep in bunuel / are women in hats, oncers, passionate
    cancers, crowns so famous bright in fossil divine, altogether,
    dee-vyne.

    D.M.Z. our initial start towards a whiteness in the kitchen
    while everyone at the dart's match
    wins more cups than Nelson
who had th'advantage of a single   eye, a
    single I

        (rain dropping,
  heavy from boughs
  under sweet sweet weight
  I stand alone
  for cups

19.

Sisyphus you are the uncool symbol of a weary age.

conspiratorial hooded pre-eminence
in spurs
makes piano any flitting moth
the golden man makes a cup an ear
because the self-propelling pirate grind
is a slow-swelling un-riverlike climate
where money's an end
(to all, too

clamp on imaginary pumps
& dance the Waltz Mephisto

20.

        Kiss you sing, <u>rache</u>, bricklayer
        or mutant bard, afraid to be established
        and afraid to die. For who deserves
     father's poppy up their nasal target derision
    o Jubilate Agno of the paranoid reveller!
   the partitions in the cafe bend a lot when I drink
     your pink
memories of a piggish evening with Yeats & a Molly Bloom.

The western hooked covenant make factory within yr chlorotic selves.

   so close I can touch your rusty red against the wall
      wait for the bell, pick up my tools, & go back.

21.

each mighty reveller has desolation in their blacksuede boots.
or just T.Rex.

22.

        In a porch of mirrors I see myself
        approaching.
          my face explodes.   Wm Burroughs says so.

    but urolagnia is no substitute for the metre-
physics of horse / cloudy
   hosts all
            & gin devours the single bead
   chalcedony
    whose daughter beryl a gem
     in each cheek
           inlaid <u>anarkhos</u>
       without paradigm.
for stealing me has become an obsession with you
a cheque book clattered in her forever opened twat.

23.

milk turned to yoghourt through double-day. I clean
up skinhead's sick (taties beer & blood) from last night's
Friday.
Up to my arms I call the landlord's wife a cunt, collect
my cards for thirteen pounds and go.

read Spinoza in the hope I'd get it right first time, next
you come in a breeze in each pore & sigh like tar
(Messiaen cymbals & horns all sleepy afternoon)

the air no keener than over a trough of any public Monday, where
I'd been inside your smile, with a hoof-masque for my head
& flowers from the heath for you, despite our normal selves

24.

  the gondola, a dichotomy of garters
because you swelled inside ecliptic time
  to show the supernovae how mighty do
the small telluric stand, rough hair & shoes

  all popped out in a vague idea of surface
  mobility

mock moon. red trees. your occultation of my rapidly escaping
 inner gasses the surest part of a general public ambivalence
towards either Horbiger & Leviticus or anyone in between

  how many arms do you have I'm told to hold
me then run off into the night
  my eyes still contain that faint green flash

25.

   The canvas is finished before you have time
   to get back in. Sneeze, and the pillar'd light
   dissolves in a warp of magnets and squid-ink

and in a breeze of disturbed ikons I finish the great
book <u>Karenina</u>, held up even as the locomotive rolled
over her body and the rail, a scarlet letter burned
into every page, hers was never quite the letter A

26.

   Red bushes. Wall damp. Latent ferocity
  streams into the vestibule walker's eyes. His
calipers seek a public death far beyond the normal
   coastal plain. His costal plan is one of debit
and mercurial asides. Hilversum wavelength! Great
  Black Shadow! Spermaceti in my lanolin bag! Tumblers
at midnight cram his exit roads, he pays no other
   price for colour and speed, and will travel far.
They move through the spectrum in a car of glass, streaked
  with the juice of loganberries. The credits roll.
you and wild aubergines fill my head with light.

Fog Eye

(1973)

in memory M.H.

The Folded Man

He is firm within
a pit of anxiety
thinly disguised
as truth. Oceans
bewray his choking
fingers, they release
his arms, literally
give him fresh
vigour, seed his
bare banks willingly.
How can he hear with
a gravestone in each
ear, so pushed from
fire he could not
name it now. Who
goes with him treads
finespun plaited
clothing so like
funeral dress. How
would he know to
adjust the dial.
Some frank teeth
will chew his soul
immortal. Clean the
step for his shoes
quicken in the final
motion towards death.

Elegy

Invulnerable nothings. Nothing
indecipherable as those ghost
messages. The seed burns by
a grey unblinking plant or moon.
You tear pages from a diary
written many years ago, but
the stories are the same today.
There are chapters like hidden doors
and they do not bear closing.
Pantomorphic sanguine rapid
books of nothings shapeless speech the
flame is not silence, only tongues.
Tired eyes, peristaltic nerve-ends
lacing. (Sun low through colonnades
and the wind with each step.)
Invest the folded man with something
as mortal as tendencies, pineal
glands fall through the awnings
in the third room of the latchwork house.
Even St. Hilda has a chisel
in her candlewick fingers, her
face streams with handcuffs
and chains. One way. It's
pressed there, more than ideas.
An irrecoverable move not quite plume
or slow-motion wing-beat.
The book, bird, flower, man, all fold up
with the approaching cumulus sudden dark.

Love Song

what's lost
irreducibly gone
who said
that some
fool bound
on passion
less omega his
senses' strange
& dormitory cares
the very plush
agony each
day he loves
an orange
tastes the
sweet
light inside

Future Dream

when sad dragons loom, the world
is wrapped inside your crumpled hand
kerchief, white
with blue edges; strange colours
shellac & bleach our former brightnesses
in great long strokes: who would I
say would you I
shout be with I exclaim
again & make the room raw; it starts
to rain, the air is a drone
of lost powers. the excited caretaker
stamps & grumbles in his latchwork
room, tries to pull off the cufflinks
he paranoically imagines chains. a quick
glimpse at last year's calendar
zeros him in on planting death in your skull;
drawn blank faces stream him along a destiny
of colour shape & sound in a dream of choiceless
parity. He wakes up only to write destiny
as density, as you walk towards the car.

Fog Eye

for Elaine

O

What could not be touched
was the will to be touched
only the fog
so usual in a basin city

the dew covers us
and we warp

how could I remember
those afternoons
hot & steamy
in the family zoo

all woodsmoke in the wind
with green wood
useless for flame

the year's end
in an obscurity of sorts

you weren't asked to go to bed
but you went anyway

E

the train
the train will
the train will have
a clear head of steam
by morning

though we warp
in the usual fog
of an obscure basin city

the dew covers us
at childhood it was hot & steamy rain
of the future

there was no woodsmoke
only the woods behind the house
were filled with it

but that's a remembrance
& I can't remember anything
only spikes
the broken wood made

the year's end
in a brash re-entry of sorts
into many forgotten things

we didn't ask to leave
but we did anyway

IL

nothing to report
but the obscuring fog
affects all static

there were no messages
but one from the past
I couldn't remember which
but you did

the buzz filled the room air
behind the house
of our future
in a basin city

the will to be touched
was a re-entry
of such quality
that the smoke dispersed

the year's end
we were asked to leave
and we had already anyway

Pelt Feather Log

(1974)

your voice
distant as
in a shell

static
breaks in
to interrupt

curbing
my tongue
in the receding
flame of your
withdrawal

"goodbye"
shortened
with a click

the receiver
snaps
into place

•

"Look, I cut me hand. Put it through a window"
"How many stitches?"
"Don't like hospitals…"

    the basement humidifier drones on
    (changing gear every hour to adjust)

    the afternoon drones on
    (flat ride long and easy to evening)

    work drones on
    (typing labels for the MacPherson Collection of Ships)

Oh to be thread-slit, pissed
next to the sky and earth's
shag back, cock rawfully

    jetting quartz pink pills
            across the black gully…

    Early world
    goodnight.

•

bright colours   acrylic tempera
poster colour water colour oil

(torn rusty shadow, bow-bone sprung
tip-deep in secret moss folds)

crying, curling, man wakes inside
the human stream, tongue out

blurts angry drone
Blue shaft stuck in eyes
"can't see anymore, only touch"

Station grey day. Inert
mask, torn and bloody.
Come home. all is white
and the wind forgiving
the flat earth stink.

•

no crown.   thorn
or gold.
beam love instead—this side
of old moon, beyond.
                    pneu
matic bovver boots. nuts
bolts gleaming oiled wrench
and rusty scaffold crown

All hazed London
from the roof

The odd passing
ship
One taller than the marine college domes!
(Russian nautical monster)

low-tide
    each keel
sinks in
    to the
rudder

Clouds move in air

•

slack day, jagged edges, lampblack
crows hovering on warm air waves
    instant death

Who
can say?
    Milk
    fills the corners
    and the room and furniture
    fold. the mild occupants
    spring up in fantastic relief.
    milk pours into sunshine
    and fills the town with cheese.

•

protocol harm. the
day breaks / time
survives the clash
of torn tongues.

    spiky
  yellow buds & thorns
    mark the even hand
      of love.

I stare into the many-faceted base
        of my cider glass
& feel the power of poetry
extending its plumed arm through my mouth!

     on the passion flower
    a spider rubs his mind
   against the world

& out from the indoor palm
 comes a hawk
   that is brightening my life

        in air

•

meeting you now isn't the same as it was.
there's a coldness in the air, chill frigid
clusters sparkle between our opposite tongues.
i walked away from you for the first time
into myself.
we both stopped but we could not see.
but i understand a little of what you wrote
centre of so much domestic quarrelling

and in this case
to endure means to walk away
each to each his separate train of events

and as you wrote all those years ago

    quite simply

       "Goodbye"

•

this fucked city
the capitol   stance
of measured argument
behind locked doors
(where else to keep
a kite but in a breathless
room)

no trains
no buses
no private means

it is a pleasure to walk
instead

(carrying a needle
pricksharp to sew up
the mouths)

starting at the hub-drone centre
and slowly spinning revolution moving out
into the amiability of sentience
past present and future

knowing i must never lose you
never drop a stitch

•

eye   and   flower
at mandala centre / drawn back
into themselves
                the Meta-Body
   first time
alone
            dolomite sandwich
            lava pie

    skim
slit   city

    pig
dies advancing

  where you lie
is how you rise

  watch your tongue swell

        in rain mist and air

•

pine residue moss tang
    "cushioning cones"

some time
   in the funnel
allow many dreams
   in your unblessed
mind

   through pinetops
madder purple writhings
   or through the ride
a purer blue

"how can you stay"

    perhaps, amber
    eyes daring eyesight
    traceries

 so high
  to be so high

•

the house is at the top of a U-valley
two miles from the sea and coves

with clearwater pools and hollowed lava
where water groans and slaps

in the evening
mist funnels up the valley
from the bay
to hide
the lowest trees

an idea of belonging returned
brightly coloured
even as much as the confused pictures
which remained clear in the mind
days after

it was a problem though, to decide / complex
knots had to be slowly unravelled

it was soon too dark and cold
to continue

the colours shifted from predominant red
through gold to purple & flashing clicking spikes of black

across the valley
a buzz-saw droned
and your shouted name
echoed around the hills

after three stops
we reached the summit
behind the house
and all problems and heat
resolved in the sea wind

•

despite the angry advancement
of colour from bracken covered hills
we fried our reason and spoke of clouds

    the weather moved around
    until mist and darkness
    slipped up the valley
    and hid even the highest trees

the backdoor light still on
moving back down, stumbling along
the forestry ride

fern   scarlet cone   spiky yellow gorse

    closing the last gate to the farm
    only the sound of running water could be heard:

•

mark the open branch pressed against the garden wall
this is your eden, among withered fruit

    trout leap against it, peach
  blossom smells its coming
    too. one leg left
  standing
on the dark valley floor

  high head
    burrowed back
  in historical guesswork / light
  buttoned by starfish wonder

    blue buds, trees
    & forests
    of your island mind

•

"throughout that whole day
warps continued
in their various conspiring forms"

even the hills opposite our resting spot
hazed over and quickly lost the flaming red
they had been all morning as we climbed
out of the lush meandering river bottom

it was a statement far beyond the implied innocence
of our ascent towards the sky / or the roe deer
startled back into pine as we ran the last way
down

we stopped   .   looked around

the centre of the earth could not be seen

•

pinned to the wall like a hooded vine.

"disruption ability
total misdemeanour
break internal icecaps
spur women to doom
(sperm in men's room)

lake cutout firewatch
stop jetting milk
leave post drop back
in ant lava puke valley
and watch the river flow"

howl like a three-legged dogbitch
as the moon ascends
and seas draw back my body into pulverised bloodiron
of the man

•

distances.

arched rock spine
pummelled by lochwater
pink larch tops against
conifer green

   "back in the Yukon
   men were ladies
   slitting pigs for real
       ho hum"

put an iceaxe steely crampon through THAT

moist brochures
of death
in coves

rime covers
all

maggots in the ram's carcass
generate their own particular heat

open yr throat
    and swallow the world

thinking of that
impossibility

•

  thin and canopied with several
translucent colours
they call you daddy longlegs.
how elegant you are
not at all priestish

only
the wind
understands you

his restless ache
wounds you
every day
clinging to the frozen frame

•

woman
stir man
me

nocturnal slit-beast moans
for womankind

crackle-smile
perfect imagery
& sound
      gentle
captor of my star-shy
animal meat

sink me
in you

in milky surfthroat
you burn
or coiling around moss
mock these illusions
& creep back
to the futuristic cave
when all dank things
are done

gulls circle
above your outward
way

we ape over rocks

lion's mane weeds
reek on lava flow
skewered by th'innocent
transparent bee

•

crackle of burning gorse.
   SMOKE BEHIND THE HOUSE!
on the fellside, crackling.

     dance
     of two young women
     one swollen with child—
     walking with new life.

    bright fresh faces
in the valley glow.

here in the city—
closed curtains, cars
revving up of a warm sunday.

eggs in a carton

skull-shell
   cracks
with noise

back there hawk and plover
make their life in air

SMOKE BEHIND THE HOUSE!

    two feathers
    floating down

•

yellow and orange daffodil
      six petals
   dotted with skydirt—
London air.

stinks even in the suburbs, cars
revving up AND TV ON.

you dry your hair
sick with almost 600 miles
driving   one day

the only driver between us.

air muck
rain grease
(oily water
runs down my neck)

yr breasts,
wet to touch and kiss
and hold the city flower
against each nipple,
steaming love.

•

warm valley air—Arran
just visible   five miles   seamist

   eagles up there
   rare bird
feathers drifting down
scared roedeer
leaping back
alarmed as us

running down
squelch of wet moss
underfoot

falling arse over head
shouting to
        WOLF IN THE SKY!

hair spun across
a hillside of purple flowers
which cannot be named

      nearest road
      two miles down
      a pitted track

chickpeas
cooking
in a pan.

northern fires
no obscurity
above the pines

      Taurus
      bending
      sniffing
      the happy wet earth ground.

•

insomnia   amnesia   blindness

total recall of three words
nothing else but supplicant
chants no poet can repeat &
SMILE

      —workt on Millwall Dock for 22 years
      couldn't stand an indoor job now. tells me
      my uncle charlie has been done for stealing
      whisky from a cargoboat ("you're not one of those
      MacSweeney bastards are you"
                        —"small world"

town:
toxic vapours
first cherry blossoms
in the squares

brickies
five floors up
eating hot sausages
fingers
dwarfing the meat

warm sunshine
gets through   up there

       three dole wallahs
       pass the emva cream
       dreaming & smiling
           in the lunchtime roar.

•

O woman
    call me stumbler

   suckt towards
   your conch
   fur   salt-sweat

mid-March
a glowing day
climbing higher and higher
up to the peak behind the house
snow
across the valley

   (pinned hawk flaps
     in singing lungs)

empty pastures
fill with shaghaired beasts

white lashes
pink pores

    on the intricate
        animal eye.

•

rock arch
arc of crotch-bone
and muscle
of thigh

running water
on the naked human body

we
  stand
    amazed
at the sight

•

city rain
is wet oily dirt—
        no friend.
the bitumen road
smells
gleams black
in its own reflected glare

rainbows
along the curve of a speeding car
hissing through the wet.

•

tubes swelling
appear this spring
through cracks

spring breaks
winter's back

six petals
on the daffodil
six centre pollen prongs
dusted yellow—
            ear
to earth.   earth
in the heart, springing
stems push through.

•

where is the god of wine and godly fuck
in all this winding desolation?   spirals
arcs   octagonal
squares
         (smeared blue
acrylic tonal pink

cock helmet swelling
red as salmon slabs

sea-salt
in polluted spawning beds

•

walking out with my wife
to check the night fishing line

      the sea
            flat
      almost a mile

    away
        across smooth rippled
    sand

sun rising
Venus
in the east
one liner
and a mirage

        two small eels
        on the line
        & all bait gone:

turning back
the illiterate worm-digger
has been there
an hour before us
and the sun.

•

Crow Pool
Wolfcleugh Hall
Hangman's Hill

    true naming
of places—

but tonight "sombre
electricity" in my head
unsure of man-put
stepping stones
across the brook, careful
order in the life
of things.

the forecast says
water-rationing
by summer.

2000 ft up the east
slope—newly melted
snow one drop
at a time down
a hollow dry fern:

    ice in shadow
cracking last.

•

bowed, bent
    face to feet, deep
folds encloak the world
    in foetal slime;
agonising pallor
    & innocent thrusts
at sky: godtrying—
    unsure of the earth
path, paleolithic
    magic/hunt of the 20th
century man in gleaming
    groves of car and
banknote glamour, stomach
    eating stomach
in the rush.

•

THE CUP THE GRAIL THE HOLLOWED BONE
AND HORN OF RAM

in which spooned-out brain
do you seek the sky
after such hysterical longing
for blind pastures

    leathered meatman, marshmallow
    trinket joy, carrots

strained & weighed, October
orange twigs to hide behind
your mind

tricks and arcs
of broken sandy light
immersed in sad rushing
water

warm sex
shadows. summer
love.   strum
the mad dove.

    beautiful wide awake eyes

    to come.

•

sad drunk
day.

pave the way
with love
let the path
wander.

steaming wine
from cups
we paint our blood
with sky

    names nouns
and adverbs to reiterate
the mewing self
regardless

i love you
    (meat
of a sweeter kind).

•

sad drunk self
mewing cloyed brain
tipped on desk
to write murder
in the vine.

were you there at ten o clock
i was

all the world was mine.
    trees bowed down
in surreal reversion
      to pale
olithic history: hunting
the grapes

     Dionysius
   drags his gleaming tool
through shining clay.

Written between December 1972 and April 1974

Starry Messenger

(1975)

for Elaine

"…I must altogether abandon the false opinion that the sun is the centre of the world and immovable, and that the earth is not the centre of the world, and moves, and that I must not hold, defend, or teach in any way whatsoever, verbally, or on writing, the said doctrine, after it had been notified to me that the said doctrine was contrary to Holy Scripture."

: Galileo Galilei, June 22, 1633, aged 70.
Extract from the confession made to the Papal
Cardinals of the Inquisition.

in a porous metal shell
sidereus nuncius
cast a V on brass water
compass against river-flow
direction mediocrity
seawards, mindwards
boxwards
behind grain
chiselled course
unslot all
there is
far from 'lyrical'
death in tepid water
evade insidious mudbores
screwing capital
down a gully
into the town of yr birth
where crabs dance
pincers raised
in razor ballet
against invading fish
& gulls

deranged flamingo
you have always flown
into the kites
of wrath
from responsibilities
abbreviated speech
annulled star-guides, rest
your flighted stutter
grace brought down
in estuary saltmud
yr peach cutlass swathed
meaning
soft as crab's
peeled easily
dabbling times

my pony guitar
sheers metal loops
into her upturned
fire-nails
flicker, punched-out
abstract childhood
& northern wheat
spewed green

my eyes began to startle
we have been magnified
my eyes to foam and forth
would recognise stars
my lips were shivering
as the levers bent forward
double of a drummer's sticks
lids of my knees crushed
blood sprang from my arms
animal fear
was not reversed
i sank
in a dream
of foes

we have been magnified
beyond all deltas
hareloops in the road
but those urban popes
killed sparrows for disturbance-technique
she is not smooth
& lunar-cool
but pitted
an enchanting planet
on bravura ellipse
in the first

tempera masterpiece
despising gallery walls
& entrance fees
coming to life
absolutely fresh
listen, frigid horn
love is a firmament
tied around
this incessant imploration

confess

my children groan
into your narrow compass
which cools the rosin
on their bow, yr devoted
friend
gathers locusts
in th'orange skirt
of her distress
Italy
foam of her eyes
& growing an oak
a voluminous loan
from nature
earth-blindness
with a partridge crown
stealing a sponge
optimistically
come to Rome

prisoner
in a stranger's
shell

naïve to the propagating ways
ellipsed in double motion
circular burning death
grow seaweed hair
regain invisibility
adopt polka disguise
clean house
for a larger crab
buck chamois
in the headlights
pufftail flashing
belts through head-high
crozier fern
guide
yourself
into the
lucid charts

Black Torch

(1978)

for Tom Pickard

Prologue

Iron & Bread
For Eric Mottram

have come from the north to feed you
iron voice brazen tongue red dust
of heart heart's unease unquiet
truth which is torn away version
inside carbonised resting black heart
in hand trees reaching left years tongue
beat inside silver river tree has
remained black unto ages visualised
streams running south to sea unfenced
tonguebeat falling inner mole black fur
fast nets fin pink rush spawning beds
go you go it has gone to the south
soft have come teeth from north east
bread is sustenance and iron   song

rain the rain poured made vines swell
grew in rain animals noise re-enter
domains of quiet noise unuse heart's
bland murder they sang always people he
remembered as a lion's mane going to work
in rain the sun made men's faces deep gold
which iron could not spa could not lustre
more moon blue in fret seen through morning
with money beyond he drinking she curled in hoops
flesh bulging goddess in red affairs events
such brilliant misdemeanours strokes along
whiteness descending scale silver blue rain falls

if you go where no one goes then shall
all of your time be spent in electric effect
as an adopted son who can run his way
but knows no course to go
      as the fair maid
      of Innerkepple
      survives
combatants to black fell blue rain
masons' handshake northern wall to Kielder
if go south is to soften the weave
undurable iron such
electric gardens tended by her when
her champions all are all in earth
her champion's scarves feet are dead *if*
they have gone no course to run or see
that there is any time so they fell and died

each word a kerbstone

Black Torch

aah travelled on the dole
sky in Tom and Connie's hair
aah cannit blame Halfden
who gave us fire
after Ida
a loathing for priests
and false fire
furred, gagged, silent
eat calm grass of islands
where fire is intended
before saddles and stirrups
southrons
pagan song drives iron
into your plaid money
you will not recall
black fire-horns
because you have none

•

the Jenny and the locomotive
        "the most important tool of progress"
    is coal
        pistons go as we recall
        reduced demand for coal
        & the fall in wages
        a recession which brought
        near-revolution
        refusal of agreements
        pits of the north east
        came to a halt

•

it varies from pit to pit
each pit has a village

men play quoits
boys (who work down the pit
stand and watch
              stoppage is almost total
              the union is the most effective
              ever seen
              in the two counties

•

thats six ton of coal yi knaa
hoo aboot that then
we had ti make a stand when we did
we ownly orn 3 and 6 a day
for six ton
aah havent orned more than 3 bob a day
in twenty yor
oh wull stay solid till the end like
till we die

•

stealing fire from the god-belly
              black dusted prometheans
              black fur of moles
              jet phlegm chalked in black dust
              white eyeballs teeth groin
              black suede tongue
              ripping fire
              from the national hearth

                      (history in fire
                      red on black
                      in Woden's
                      name

•

management say the men earn over 3 and 6 a day
the union denies it
their lawyer says it is not true
it is only 2 bob a day
pitmen everywhere should be paid more
they are asking for 28 per cent

its impossible to offer it
we cannot guarantee sales
an increase of this sort to men injured in the pits
would mean more men pretending injury
its already up to ten shillings a week
why should he be able to stay on in his pit cottage
when he is disabled out of work and therefore non-productive

•

aah keep a door
          in Evan Jones's pit
but aah'l never
          get used tiv it

foremen become shareholders
union leaders look at gold watches
picked for the board
token folk
moved into houses
with indoor netties
wives pour tea
and fidget in the new presence
at xmas they give charity
reversing 30 years

•

wages paid weekly
security of tenure
minimum 15 bob a week
widows pensions increased

injury payments increased
they earn almost as much as factory workers
the families are able to eat meat every day
all have gardens

•

nee schools or churches
so miners set up their own
a close-set community
at one aah get me breakfast
half an hoor ti get inbye
the bent wark
hew on ya honkas coz theres nee room
yi get used tivit
ten tubs a day
wor bairn leaves the hoose at half past 3
13 yor owld
gets yem at five
at neet
he gets 1 and 3 a day
his little bit meks aal the difference
he gans to the rantors school
the kids should be trained by wor folk
to lorn the proper things for working people

•

not Halfden
    not these men who lacked true control
    "whelps from the lair"

    these others
            curs
    dogs in the city
    kennelled
           in velvet

> *children moaned as their fathers*
> *brothers and uncles were brought out on stretchers*
> *of wood and cloth*

invented to serve
      & die
   dogs & curs
without names

hidden deep in Ponteland

pillaging in the city
      invisible

  now watching
  from a cell

•

hes ownly got one suit
sav got one frock
aah went to the master's hoose
he keeps his wine in a bigger place
than we live in!

lord londonderry
former emissary to Austria
an eminent tory
it is a contract that reflects
the obligations

regular work
a decent home
as an obligation to hew coal
i have honoured my obligations
and more
i have risked a fortune building
seaham harbour
to ensure the transport of coal

•

it is slavery

•

30,000 miners on Blackfell
resolved not to go back
until demands are met
    we are degraded
    we produce the wealth
    & the coal on which wor future rests

    di ye dine on pheasant & wine
    we are determined to be free
    are their wives widowed by the pits
    we have the unity to brek the bond
    the long night of tynnary and slavery is ower

•

after the omniverous mart
        "marten beaver and squirrel"
where portly merchant
            characteristic
    of the north armerican trapper

    Henry III
    supplied a charter
    to the townsmen
    of Newcastle

    so they may
    dig
    for fire

    in the wake of Ida

    for coal

•

why were the pits left idle for so long
they profit from the shortage
coal prices rose 20 per cent
we had stocks when the strike started
naturally a shortage will make prices rise
how much profit did they make during the strike
the price was high
are you really suggesting we should have stopped selling
what coal we had
this so-called union has misled the simple men
who refused the bond
am i to agree to wages that would ruin the trade
this union
this stupid strike
i won't lift a finger

•

strangers arrived in northumberland and durham
the pits slowly but irrevocably started to turn
the strike has begun in earnest

•

you are sulphur
breathing
beneath black forests
of the past

"Newcastle's very well-considered system
of municipal government"   charters
granted   not taken   for granted   liberties/that
is   removed
                naked aborigines of Tyneside
                wading for salmon and char
                70 yares of the Stanley Delta
                owned by Cuthbert

and the See of Durham
one is common   fished
by blond natives
who are more efficient
along the north banks

    (before
common land was
captured
by mitred brigands
armed with falsities
of Bede

    Tyneside
        iris
        of the island

        down
        rivers

        to the
        sea

•

the union is rumoured to be wealthy
run by chartists
its own rallying point a newspaper in newcastle
the strongest
it lobbied parliament
to force up wages
they pay for their own lecturers
   because we have been ignorant
   these lies have been repeated to the miners

   23 strands broken
   out of 96
   they had ti gan back doon
   there was nee light
   someone brought a lamp

woosh! yi bugga
they fund their bones
on the heap next day

a hundred yards away

•

the owner sd bring the horse oot first
thats what theyre like
we break arms and legs
or get sick
black dust doon ya lungs
en yiv had it
weve carried them oot unconscious
oot for 15 weeks and nee pay yi knaa
his cough eeh the doctor says
he'll always be bad
ut never gets loose

•

yes
there is a certain percentage
of bronchitis
breathlessness can be treated by a change of air
yes
you would think it is injurious to their health
but coal dust as far as i can see
seems to have no adverse effect at all
coal is vegetable in origin
therefore it is organic
therefore unharmful
that is scientific truth

•

no energy compromise
                          smoke LOCK-OUT tobacco until

        death of energy
        circled in your selves
        one unanimous vote

as I have recorded
they float around the meniscus on a raft of weeds

        that the See of Durham
        represented, initiated and actively partook
        in fierce accumulation of common land
        this warlike custom laid the base
        of ecclesiastical capitalism
        in northumbria
        and the church's vast collection
        of properties, in other words
        profit
            without work

1279
    a verdict was returned
            the priors of Tynemouth
and Durham
        had erected towns on either side
of the Tyne
        "where no towns should stand"
to the great injury of the whole borough
and had also made a brewery at Sheles
where only boats should be
            whereby
              the borough lost its furnage
in the employment of bakers' ovens
amounting to fourpence in every quarter

the sentence was
        clear and simple: no towns

            on the Tyne

            save Newcastle.

•

dog-eyed Pearl
ya mutha's mad
scabby hill-witch
humped by village drunks
not served in shops
gets ya springwater
along the top road
buckets full of slop
Pearl first girl
i saw naked
and ran aged 6
swimming in the trout pool
at Blackbirds Ford
local tykes
blocked ya chimney stack
with slate slag
house choked wi smoke
no one helped
bastard daughter
of a witch
we said
but you were interbred
crossed-eyes
& dog-tongue
stiff with fear

then aa heard
ya mam died
& you were put
inside

•

they fined him 3 and 6 for losing a shovel
yi can buy one for 2 shullin in the shops
ti put ya tally on the tub
ti tell wees done it
the keeker at the tub

puts it in his back pocket
he gyps yi the bastard
ya working for nowt
after ten hours they tell you theres stone
aah said aahv got clean coal
the buggas gan on like that aal the time

•

fining is at the owner's discretion
they are fined more than ninepence a day
the inspector is hardly impartial
dining on salmon and beef

•

we would much rather employ local men
but we have no choice
until the men come to their senses
i did not expect it to go on as long as this
it is the fault of the chartists

the pit prop holds the roof & gives support
we support the master when we work
so when the prop breaks
we break their profits

•

the pitmen's lecturers say
the masters are afraid of the solidarity of this strike

•

balance out of synch   swimming in fragments
we smoked LOCK-OUT tobacco   STRIKE tobacco
I wanted BLACK TORCH beer

                promethean moles
                under the earth
                the hearth
                the heart
                away from platonic misogynists
spongey cloak encrusting

city well-gutted   Georgian crescents ripped
back alleys gouged   holes in centre cells
spaghetti roadway experimental roundabouts
metro stations into the city crust   breathes
freshness, advancement, progression, okay

the year of Dan Smith and Alderman Cunningham

•

the master lays on special trains
bringing up strangers
from wales
wee says there's 500 gannin back
they put them stories oot to weaken wu
this village is solid
every union man is oot

•

blacklegs walks past the pickets
howay noo lads
divven gan in man
think aboot the union
didnt yi see the notices
tellin yi not to come
aam tellin yi
aam ownly tryin to explain
if we can win here
you can win in Wales
how wid ye like to be fined
for havin stone in ya coal

gan back man
aav got a wife an kids an all
stand by is man
divvent let them buy yi
wi tokens
its you we're fighting for
howay man
        gan back

•

bell-pit carter chain and girdle   "the skip
was too heavy to pull"   levels filled
      water   windlasses jammed

        fortunate than
           her head, warm clothing

      not as 1840
      Walter Coffin
      at Dinas
      employed 8-year-olds
      both sexes
      under-nourished
      could not read
      pulling trams
      no holidays
      2 ½ pence a week
      running forward
      over the unfortunate boy
      "the train broke through
      the door"

            five   hundred   weight
      of coal
      plus
      the weight
      of a skip
      others
      had no wheels

and were dragged up shafts
to baskets
"I have not been hurt yet"

this
frequently happened, killing
the workers, their children

•

lord londonderry will not talk with the union
it would be pointless
i will negotiate with my own men pit to pit
otherwise it is impossible
i am a kind and indulgent master
they are infatuated with this union
it is a rabble
led by radicals and revolutionaries
should i speak with them

•

we've not had a man arrested since december
we've never lost a case yet
wor leaders do what we say
and wor better off for it

•

primitive methodists
are the ones
with their evangelism
who have kept the men out
for so long

•

who carried a wicker cage
            which held a shining

blackbird /
> "the rats run away with my bag sometimes. I wash myself clean…"
>
> (Morgan Davies 1840 aged 7

lusty black chanter
smell after gas
flap flaring wicks
die to protect
black-dusted brothers
mouths tobacco black
hockle jets spew
crude lamps make it gleam
before dust chokes the colour

no trumpet sweet-throat flourish

all shafts lead to hell.

•

pitmen's families feel the effects
women illegally pick coal from heaps
the strike is peaceful and disciplined
by July the families face further deprivation
   eviction
strangers take their cottages
pick the shiny bits mind
divvent pick flint
it doesn't burn

•

we pawned the dresser
candlesticks
me wedding ring
the ornaments
everybody has

•

no one will use any violence
there's 30,000 of us
and if we stick together
they can do what they like
we'll win in the end

•

if you get the intellectual notion
                           of coal
    there will be a filthy
  armchair theorist
                hewing carboniferous seams
                Beamish and Mickley

        Montague & Rokeby
        poets
        hunted newts
      flashy
      over bark

    beyond Hartfell
                spines knot
  under millstone
    iron & lead

        coal
            nearer the sea
                on a final shelf

            is 280 fathoms at Pemberton's Colliery
        under magnesian
             into the German Ocean

            (there are signs
          on
          the map

•

i reasoned with them
i pointed out their folly
i was reasonable
they were stubborn
obdurate
i have endured this strike
until my patience is exhausted
now his majesty
and his rights of property
must be protected

•

the bailiffs
are yi ganna wark
  yi knaa better than that man
then get them oot
  bairns crying
  mam mam
  whet they deein
  aw be quiet pet
bailiffs clanking pots
busting the furniture
  nee violence
  fagodsake hev yis not done enough
  yu fuckin gets yi bastads
  aal fuck you aal fuck you
  its alreet pet its alreet
  the army stands ready
  to howld the peace

•

they divvent give yi any chance
we havent got much to start with
they smashed everything we had
and thats not much

the lass is bad there man
get a shovel
howay man
put a smile on ya face
give them a hand
we'll get the bairns to relations
but they're 20 miles away
oh it's alreet pet
the strike'll soon be ower

•

Grainger Market
    hecatombs of fresh killed meat
 poachers
    dealers in rabbit
  from Hartfell Alston Allendale
    Cowshill
        and Sparty Lea
  alive and dead
   flush beaks pocked
with shot from Blaydon

 peahen leveret stag
 salmon gaffed in Coquet
 blind brown trout from Teams

  fighting cocks
    and cards
 try the patience
   of the searcher
in the Brass Man
and the Anchor which fell

"the people are like coal
      in mortar"

   Butcher's Spitoon
   Lam Burn
     Execution Dock

    wooden cobble cross
    at Gallowgate
            to Eldon Square
    whose founder
            stole from Shelley

    then the moors

       Jedburgh Ayrshire and Fife

•

be ye also patient brethren
the lord draweth nigh
he'll grant our success
and wreak his vengeance
let us say a prayer
to establish our resolve

•

"this kind of teaching does not help the men
to ignore the ranters and chartists"
encampments are springing up
over the two counties
survival to win the strike
hinges on their strength
against poverty and the elements
on the moors
they didn't care what they broke
the bairns think it's a bit of an adventure
we have some flour
we shared it out
we get the odd rabbit
poached from the park
we eat nettles
i divvenaa what we'll dee aboot tomorra
they've even diverted the streams so we cannot get water

•

25,000 miners met in Newcastle
but evictions continued
local magistrates are convinced
violence is inevitable
it has been minimal so far
due to the discreet presence of troops
the owners have already resorted
eviction
troops
special constables
   we thought we had a fair claim
   we were trodden on
   we should have fought for the pits
   wi shovels and fire
   we live on nettle broth
   i thought you said god was on wor side
   he is man
   he is
   well aah wish the buggah would tell the owners

•

where beds of black torch
          reach magnesian limestone
     last of the shelves
        german ocean
     there the boats are
200 miles of blockade
Eyemouth Blyth
     at Tynemouth and Shields
    whole of the Tyne fleet
         by far the strongest vote
no other vessel used the tides all day
in or out
         but one
on the condition it returned to Bergen
subsidised cod still in the freezer-hold

   an injunction has been applied for
      so scab fish can enter the nation

•

   there'll be no pit justice
until the pits
are in the hands of the real owners
the pitmen

Melrose to South Shields

    black quilts
        black torch
    salt tears standing
    she fair flower
       water swam with speed
loup for rough hills
      perilous Farnes
star-haunted Ida
      presenting fire
not drowsing south
      storm & glade music
storm is lord
    & midnight evil-starred
breaking in foam
    Coquet Font & Tyne

•

if the Scald offends
      rigorous law
    exile him to Deadwater

where he can be real
among real laws, or Maiden
Way where
millstone
is too hard to hew

        send him a barren seat
        at the head
        of Houxty Burn

        where anger
        is Ida
        fire

(& the priest's
flame
is blind

•

we must end this strike
as soon as possible
we have only been cruel
in order to be kind
the pitmen must act
as if they are a wayward child
and come back to work

•

all the workers needed for the pit have been acquired
blackleg non-union scab travellers

the pitmen returned
they had won nothing

•

they've never done nowt for wu
they always took and never gave
that's what they're like aal the time
aah dug coal hewing the guts of earth
providing fuel for the hearths of millions
an what divva get fuck all that's what
ahv worked ten oors a day for forty yor
me lungs are tight aah can hardly breathe
aah cough at neet and can barely sleep
me sons are doon the face knee deep in water
rippers at ashington like aah was at Stanley
cramps arthritis me left hand froze one winter
aah used ti play darts and bowls
now it's all aah can de ti lift a pint
you get depressed like when you divvent work

aal them years then have them kick yi oot
they say ya too sick to work and cannot bend
yi cannit lift a pick to hew the top coal
they say ya too shaky and cannit be trusted
me mates knaa aam a good lad and de me bit
it's for them aam sick and they treat yi like muck
they always say one thing and de another
aam sick alreet but it's not me lungs it's me spirit
aahv been whipped aah may as well get used tiv it

•

I was at yor hoose last neet, and meyd myself very
comfortable. Ye hey nee family, and yor just won man
on the colliery, I see ye hev a greet lot of rooms,
and big cellars, and plenty wine and beer in them,
which I got ma share on. Noo I naw some at wor colliery
that has three or fower lads and lesses, and they
live in won room not half as gude as yor cellar. I
don't pretend to naw very much, but I naw there shudn't
be that much difference. The only place we can gan
o the week ends is the yel hoose and hev a pint. I dinna
pretend to be a profit, but I naw this, and lots o ma
marrows na's te, that wer not tret as we owt to be,
and a great filosopher says, to get noledge is to naw
wer ignerent. But weve just begun to find that oot,
and ye maisters and owners may luk oot, for yor not
gan to get se much o yor own way, wer gan to hev some
o wors now . . .

                    letter left by a pitman in the
                    house of a colliery viewer in 1831
                    into which he and his mates had
                    broken during a strike riot

•

black middens & dusky holds
    Stella chews the atmosphere
  Lemington and Scotswood
        to Wallsend
where Roman barriers resigned ground
     not furnishing the world with toys
     and trinkets to dismay
Titans in a hammer glow
        dark lords
     of storm and political tides
     Roman sentries dreaming of Naples
     pulled down by long hooks from the wall
     as Alaric approached the gates
            of the seven hills
    there have been straight roads through Newcastle
    & household gods
                Mithras
                & the Raven Banner

            mix in the blood of children

            from the eye
            an island can see
            the edge of its axe
            or the fames of its natives
            under sail

Black Lamp Strike

Luddism ended
on the scaffold   Marcus Despard Jeremiah Brandreth
militia-gored
street-dragged   to Southwark stretching an illegal
tradition
Masked Orator   harangues in midnight shire fields
letters from
distant societies   burn them with candles
Drag the Constitution
from its hidden place   attend Black Lamp's penumbra treason
joined to Black Torch
& Black Torch Strike   chains of seditious affection
8 subdivisions
in Southwark alone   Flower's marauders   letters
swapped at
heifer marts   fenland cornsheaves stuffed with Paine
Cambridge Intelligencer
farmyard sedition   solidarity *with* transformed
solidarity *against*
'stretch & fetch'   brave motto   *Facts are seditious things*
corruption facts
poetry facts   complete dominion over the fruits
our sickle
our bread   England's root-fed hordes
Tom Paine
in a cubby   'on the sly'   hidden quarto volumes
under Welsh
hillside boulders   candlelit gangs of Glamorgan

& Denbigh
gods stand amazed   Combination Acts are tail-eating snakes
clustered groups
fiercer focus   fustian-cutters   Blackburn cotton spinners
calico-printers
woolcombers   journeymen from various trades & towns
facts are
seditious things   printing names & misdeeds publish addresses
advertise
lies   they break into pieces this
haughty wand
resolve against   slayers of widow stranger fatherless son
facts
make fragment   flaming upward straight mischief
condemn
innocent bloods   rock and refuge   families combined
abilities
known   shall cut them   through the people's hands

Black Torch Sunrise

"Who can live with this Consciousness
and not wake frightened at sunrise?"
—A<small>LLEN</small> G<small>INSBERG</small>

BBC monochrome newsreel flickers
   jerking on small family tv screen—
 Sorbonne students hoy parking meters
   paving stones ripped, military phalanx
lowers grinning plexiglass
bodies' confrontation on sensual Paris boulevards
   tolerated hash in Amsterdam cuts down riot-quota

  "our correspondent says there will be no
 repetition of the 1968 near-revolution
  because students have not gained support
 of the French working-class"

Leftists mount insurrection
    neat covert agents ensure safety
  When does "made payments"
     become "offered bribes"?
Will the Labour party uphold the jailing of pickets?
Of course.

—TUC inner cadres make closed door pacts with the Govt
This allows the £
    some relief on the European market
  Bank of England dwarfs
 up the lending rate
  affording confidence
    to other dwarfs/

Circles broken circumferences ripped
   perimeters buckled
  facts revealed
    must be published
  because they are seditious

Dragged by the hair students
               on *Daily Telegraph* page one
    suitable captions
       of a certain persuasion

"Days lost in strikes are the lowest
            in seven years
      The people of Britain are determined
           to beat inflation"

Whipped legs
     of left-bank women students
         blur on the shimmered screen
         625 line consciousness—
  systems of response have woven into them
   a right to decide on issues
   pertinent to individual consciousness, local energy
          & mass development

      —plugs are juice-taps
          inside skirting boards

     overalled workers come on shift
        in Scottish grid complexes—

"At three minutes past eight you must dream"
      Sir John Gielgud/
               Lee J Cobb dead, Sal
   Mineo dead in Hollywood suburbs
  alleys exploded liver burst
     mugger's dark blade

   elegiacs & glittering heroes
   sour with mediocre filmwork

"There is work and there is art. So far all
   I have done is work—you could say
     I feel bitter about that"

    Lee J Cobb in manly cowboy snarl
     20 years after *On The Waterfront*
     & Sinatra paid his debts

 no revolution repetition on the hour
  les flics keep low profiles
    hooligan is an easy word to use in Paris
     for the gauchistes
     as is sincerity
 when referring to the obedient athletic policemen

   Bird, bat or strangling Reynard
   wheeps in the graveyard
   domestic cats snarl at window-sill
   through leaves & long-grass

How many fantasy robot women
     of university poets
    have "coral-branch" limbs
     breasts "full of secrets"?

   Breasts are for kissing
   & for bairns' milk
   a lovely touchable part
   of both sexes

  these poets take to bed
     wind and water—monochrome opposites
   of reality's many shades

   —pine matches burn
     in coal
  flare because
       parts of the wood
      remain worthy of fire, like a poet
       growing older.

   Winds of southern dawn
    blow vermilion gases
     in my skull.

        Barbiturate environment!
        Marshmallow urbanity!

          Newcastle poets
    aim pearl-inlaid shotguns
    on Allendale & Nenthead fells
      heads down behind
           desolate lead workings
        where John Martin
           looked in terror on the pitman's lamp

        Bunting translates Catullus
          in Wylam
        old as the century.

Pickard lams battered arts council grant landrover
        into cathedral snowdrifts
            on bitter dale hillspine—

        rural economics are a laugh
          if you don't compensate
            for snow.

        On the hour every hour
        Paris correspondent reiterates
        his dirge—snow dances
            by itself in Northumberland
        & doesn't recognise farmers.

Newcastle helicopters fetch emergency cowcake and hay.

    Pondwater wine stinks
        raw meniscus on wrists
  Less hair on head of husband
        ageing quicker than clocks tick

    You chuckle in sleep
        blissfully away
    from aweful consciousness

            for a few hours—I stare at you
            in this dark
            which is like a hurt, afraid
                                for your safety
        alone.

        I deal in secret financial reports
            confidential manpower utilisation documents
            council Deep-Throats with secrets to tell
        I must protect my sources
                to weld Press trivia
            in low-key suburban rags.

                    Obvious conflict for a poet
                        in this predicament—

                        to be worked out
                            as it goes
                            & as it falls
                            to be cleaned.

Foot stretched out sleepy cramp alone
    Cooling coals crack and shift
            in London hearth—Real miners
    ripped that coal—to chuckle
            in your sleep, wife, is better than shaking
                at sunrise / solitary

                    chic rocking chair
                    slowly hisses
                                to a stop.

                    Baroque mandolins
                        plucked music
                            before the next normal news from Paris.

Uncollected Poems

(1980–1990)

Jury Vet Told: Come Back and Learn the Way

Into the Dangerous DECADE . . . . . .

      she was the garbo gone. stuffing mindglue blown,
vlix bangings wagged, born on a river, bankless,
         how she did it.

      she did it real, nowhere special, messaging
outwards, coloured madder rose iron when
      Shoes Burned In Her Hair of Rings
THESE WERE HER THINGS & HOLES.

Salt on her renaissance table dried up, blocked heartenings,
    hailed & solitary from each pore
      Where Society hangs loose.

In the 1980s we shall have to find some fairly urgent solutions.
          (QUOTE)

      you loved my black & purple primrose badge
        dedicated to The Passions
          on a grey wool v neck
             worn
        ACROSS THE HEART

Yr. boots too short. Wool & fur. Suede
      scuffed in mudlicking
        grimness
      borne in solitude
          Muckings crudette
which splash & sting.

    To rest is golden brooch.

But to change is a Ring.

With a lapus starlet sneaking in corners to smile
AT ME.

Ode Antique Tongue

Have ye beheld (with much delight)
A red-Rose peeping through a white?
                    Herrick

THY AZURE ROBE
I did behold
as ayrie as the leaves
of
gold.

I will punish thee.
Throw
wet
stones.

Wound with thy dart
O TART
of street & slime
& SLUM.

I
seek the
freshly
laundered lawn
pulled
up
into
a starry
sight
of
Thee.

What brave vibrations
sparking happiness!

You eat their lusciousness.

I have sniffed
the hiprose &
smarting
Briar
too
.

Lace nylon Cups,
clothing so abrupt.

In the dark none dainty
I kiss yr Shoes.

! EACH TOE A RED & WHITE ROSE !

Carve Her Name with Pride

for Virginia McKenna

MULLET WINDOWS (spheres almondine
reached up nylon trunks
of peach-tinted light) : I SEEK
YOUR FLUTTERING SHADE!

Trenched cress, GLOBES to the root,
lined with cups & POOLED.
Thus
fooled,
each antique
serf
of love & scribe & wing.

BEND
yr feathered
bone
into sight of her.

Deter is death:
snake lips, merchant grin
chalked on
creamy thighbone lust.
KISS IS CRUST.
Trust,
you say, lunging
at the stile
beneath an ornament of
clouds.

Rain & husbandry disastrous
to a core of green.

Her each wing do stamp marks
of gold
upon my silver brow.

Madame sharkette, petite gudgeon
is a filthy stream of wounded pulsing
queens. Tilth is friable
to any burning shoe. Glabrous
carmine toenails, I have
munched your lunch
of flesh & NOW
I'M FREE TO CHOOSE

Gasp for a fall from grace.
salt on wounded
legblood, hounded
by her saline face.

Crisp in sheets of glass, he
parts each furrow down: betrayed
the rudegirl stamps her soul
cool.

BRACKEN IS HER DREAM OF STEEDS
How can we know dolls.
Or dusty teddybears.
for WISTERIA MADNESS on each breast
gives sullen
charm
to that cooling brengun
mind.

We pay in kind.

She is Aella's bride,
killed & conned & whisked
by storm
in brutal streets
of
mortar dust.

TO LIVE IS LUST.
TO DIE IS SHAME.

YOU HAVE BEEN CULLED

& the green island

is nerveless,

THICK WITH BLOOD.

Blood Money

for Tom Pickard

Conspiracy drugged
arsehole rat, you
are the hook
on which we live.

Ghastly human engines,
so deviously combined
& sucking up to tabloid change.

We eat the daily
page one rage.

Venom on the plastic
counter ticks away
with time.

Workers on trial
crawl in drones
down conduits
& telephones.

Dad, give me broth.
Let me suck the bone.
Dad, give me heat.
Dad, dad, where's your head?

Dad, let me drive
the situation home.
I don't want it anymore.
I want to be free.

There is no justice. Only
sexy cash, horny fivers & tens
pour from every woven Burton sleeve.
Sweaty greasepalm

masons' handshakes
in the mayoral parlour NOW.

Dad, they're beating my knuckles
with sticks. I'm bruised. My nose
feels like a stone.

While Benidorm's bartills swell
with bent councillors' backhanders
& civic officers on the make.

Don't tell me mate, I KNOW.
It's all
bought fannies, boss rodents,
covert pens in booths,
porno felt shoe bees, headblood's
cushy lifelong puking
on the catfood ground.

Dad, my soul is rusting
away. It tastes like salt.
It's horrible.

Feral edges scraped & raw,
blistering bollocks
raked by acid windrain.

No cosy coal comfort,
blacking people sucking
up their caustic. Bind

citizens with zimmer
frames cowering on
pathways in gritfilled

precincts, putting up
with the NEDC's new
housing deal. City

dwellers in queues,
waiting for nothing.
Dad, the pickets are

standing outside but
no one is listening.
It's a silent movie

in a madman's mind.
From Castle Tower down
to every grubby lintel

it comes, mapless, armed
with locust architects,
mantis lawyers, gliding
Porsches and unpunished
deeds.

Dad, I checked my watch
and it said: this is
ZERO TIME.

Don't tell me, mate.
I KNOW. It's all
Ponteland bungalows
& new Cortinas, kiddie's

riding lessons, Maltese
hospitals for Reggie Maudling's
mob, suntans for the wife
while we screw Newcastle

on the clubhouse bunker
at Gosforth Park, and the sun
over Dan's Castle glows
on a thousand gin and tonix

from here to the Civic Centre.

Don't tell me, mate.
I KNOW. It's all
pimp ties fuming,
blood money whipping
hands, children
who inhabit & inherit
this city dread. Tory

lunching Labour conmen
at the Turk's Head, I'll
have quail & Burgundy, what's
in it for me stuff. Jesmond

bints humping venomous
blackmail goadlust, armed
with Polaroids & cured clap.
Crassly starlit eyebrows

pigging halves of lager
at the Haydon Bridge Hotel
in the tinkling tinsel
bastard snow.

You'll get yours JackJim
Fred Pearl SuntannedLilly
You'll get yours Isabel
Norman Frank and John.

THAT'S AFTER I GET MINE.

REVULSION (Torvill & Dean)

1.

        Through Albion's collapsed & mental tones
                    there's This:
                        body
                        heat
        and angry jolt blood bugle. Fine
                        horn
                  exterminating
                       Ghosts.

                       Vesta
          jazzing toots profonde,
                    pasting
           figjuice lifenodes.

              Tail's a gronfer,
                   blazed
             wreckjobs flak
                    each
                    Sled.

                  Go to,
              she says &
                  Utter
                  Cool:

                  Fling
              your blue
                      &
              make my
                  Burnt
            Sienna Real.

SO HARMONY RAPS & RAIDS BEYOND THE EDGE
WHERE CRAWLERS
TILT & DOLL & DO
THEIR
UTMOST TO
CONFORM.

Uniformly, bale-juice,
lickspit.
All the meccano poets,
fleeced with stale.

Gasjets pleat the day.
Spleenjots flake us daily.

2.

We are BIG SHAME IN SHOES.
We suck at Girocrawl.
We graffiti Giants.
We subway soul.

We Meat Puppets,
Black Flag.
We Xerox New York.

We mincing debs.
We hot magazine cover.
We tool room Charlies
aching for a
Load
of Zero.

We docking in Albion's
trash bays
and redundant rivers
Armed with
gliffs of vicious

Wordbone.

We rotarblades and harmony
breakers,
stolen
reward smashed from
its plate.

WE THE HEADY BOUNCETONE!

We gang sequence,
throwing up on Fancy
Dan
&
fellow
traitors
in the swamp,
or any social worker's
basement
squat.

We Natalie Wood swimming
lessons.

Let's rewrite the
News!

Be fabjolt,
spine shudder warning
crazed mockery hoyed with speed,
flick-pinnies waved in
awe: go

mad without Prize.

3.

    We fact sheen charm.
    We the chained.
We break our lives and bleed.

      We go without.
    We rarely feast in full.
We trade treasured beasts for
        favours.
    We misunderstand
      every visitor.

We blame the bairns.

   We beat the wife
     and she
       goes
      home
    without
    apology.

We live alone.

———

We walk the crazed paving
        &
  NEVER FIND THE
    GARDEN.

———

We bet and lose in
   silence.
We cater for resentment.
  We paint the walls
   and never
call it Home. We

look at ancient photographs
and live inside
their distant
Rim.

We drink and drink
playing perfect
Host
to all that's fucked.

We watch favourite cities
in decline.
We get the 125.
We leave behind the
black & white.
We marry blondes.
We make incredible mistakes.
We look for love
and end up blighted.

4.

YR BEAUTY IS ENHANCED, YOU ARE
OKAY.

O fathom it, whipsheen. Fling
thus tall
what's brightest,
as if another place.

Wing tote.
Flex brain.

Terrific silk's what
smooths the
chaps.

———

DRENCHED WITH IT: life.

DRENCHED WITH IT: blood.

NOT DONE WITH IT: ever.

---

honeybeat jamming flitblades, yes.
Joy mammoth fiendwords.
Yes.
Definitely cliffedge tele
grams.
Heart stadium engine burn and
despair like a glove.
Frisklamb yearnings.
Leapsmiles.
Poembirth from terror
brainburst.

Mozart's soulturning tides and
Schubert's beckfall.

Yes, yes, yes.

DRENCHED
AND DUNCHED
WITH
IT

&

Never Done.

5.

　　　Hot pursuit, head alive in books.

　　　　　Albionic jaw:

　　　era of collapsed hopes,
　　　resurrected pain-triggers,
　　　　　belted Zeros,
　　　　tongueless bells,
　　　　thriving attacks,
　　　beast fun jamborees,
　　　　　hypothermia,
　　cut bodies and windscreen
　　　　　　Romance—

　　　all a misting of suns
　　　　where we trace
　　　　　the Blame
　　　　　　　or
　　　　lamely write in
　　　　　　Steam:

　　　Drenched with It
　　　& Never done.
　　　　———————

　　　　Cool, not cold.
　　　　Writ sharp.
　　　　Housed in slate
　　　　　and stone.
　　　Bathed in fernsoap
　　　　　　&
　　　　Hung with
　　　beads and gems.

　　　　Fashioned by
　　　　　desyre &

Hopeful
lost
in Aire,

skins aflame with
Drenchblood.

Drenchblood pulsegraphs
jerking,
as we ascend all buff
and pinkytrots.

We nimblefinger to the grave.

We thighblue meander
down her sapphire
veins.

We dancing in the dark
alone.

6.

We locked out
in
street wet
but Harping just
the same.

———————

Drenchtones fuming:

liquid savage
rumbles,
frank teeth,
immortal tendencies,
hip fury twanged,
zest curtains,

SPEECH TRACKS LIT BY STARRES.

Drenched
with it and
Never

<u>Done.</u>

State of the Nation Bulletin January 85
for Maggie O'Sullivan.

Soft Hail

For what
it's worth
he carried
his shield
high, yet
loved her
stupidly—
a welter
of words
fired by
alcohol:
achieving
nothing.
Would he
win her
back with
that gust
of verbals,
as she was
(his mistake)
in doldrums
in raw
upland
country—
of Hadrian
and Bede,
of peewit
and coal
smoke rising—
wanting
her attentive
to sudden
roars of
his own
nature?
Disturbed

by variance
of becks
and tides
they crossed
swords
in a time
when guns
were fashionable:
leaned on
one another
when
the fight
was done.

•

That black
rag crow.
A dry
stone wall
whose
solidness
has
seen off
generations.
Including
you, muck
spreader.
And you,
professor
of
agricultural
research.
(A florin
lost beneath
that stile
going for
Nichol's eggs
when time

did not
seem hard).
Now it is
insane grubbing,
like Büchner's
Lenz, clawing
borage root, arguing
with blackthorn
for space
and sharpness.
Under parliament
of birds
he tramps miles,
salt-lick
in a bag
and knack
for skin-stripping.
That crow
again. Here
northern end
of empire.
Here
the mind
tramps about, but
the heart stays put.
The rest—if
it could
be said—is
silence.

•

Last night—
was she on
Red Crag?
Mewing in
a bitter
wind—con-
testing

blackthorn
and gorse,
arguing
relentlessly
with absent
birds, fingering
bracken
in wild
distraction:
alone in a copse,
married now
to other gales
and storms.
She might
seek quietness
in shaft or byre,
still broken
by weather perhaps—
rag-rotten
queen of troughs
and silage, cloakclasp
barely pinned,
lodged in a sike
where grandness
reigned: blood
high as
her true
station.
We punish
the earth
its refusal
to settle
unreasonable
demands, as
if it could.
Heartless,
we are divided
in ditches,
under stars.

•

God, all
that moorland
gossip
of curlew
and quail
you say
you love
as if you
did not
love me.
Like you,
it is
stone walls
out here.
Barriers
across
hard
country.
I cannot
find, hard
man, a grid
to cross
to you.
Before leaving
lowlands
for this windswept
common
we mewed
under sheets
like breeze
over becks
and burns.
Hiding in
laughs, why
don't you
love me
as I should
be loved? Plover
loves you, why

can't I?
Showing me
such storms
and squalls
bought in
a bottle—
frankly, it
is unpleasant.
Yet I am
shrugging,
wiping
my eyes,
trying to
find you
again.

•

In land
of cow clarts
you loved me
strong and long,
and you took
my breath away.
What were
those
tribe dues
unpaid?
And those
water rights
and fencing
disputes?
O but
I loved
your northern
eyes
before you
lashed me
with spit,

before you
flashed silence
at me, before
you drove
me out.
I loved you
on that
foggy cleugh,
hugged your
armour against
sad sores,
among the
tumbled stones.
Hay reek
not used to
pig's urine,
blood on
your boots.
Often I was
ashamed
to be alive.
Then we made
grand hay
ourselves.
Love, love
me again,
cool the
ache: bring
one another
from the
edge of
the world.

•

You go
into
the nothing
night

and walk around.
Funny fixtures
glow
and gleam.
Jetstream—
more Geordies
off
to Spain.
Stand
in rows
of kale
with temper
and cleaver
to match,
watch
her berate
the lawnmower
not doing
its job.
You go
into
the nothing night
mind
clicking
past snaps.
In the
house
a hooley,
but you're
not there.
Nothing else.

•

She
returned—
curlew
whooping
over gorse.

The wind blew.
He faced
the gale.
Plovers rose
and resettled
and he
humped
his bag of stones
door to door.
Cats dead,
dog-tired,
sheep in another
fold. Fury
took peculiar
turns: polite
postcards,
phones
hammered down.
There were
no redeeming
qualities.
Now the
day's hard stare
beckons on.
Her letter
on the mat.
Fifty five
words. Snow
falls and
the hatches
are down.
No exit.

•

Gathering
kindling
in a lowland
Saxon copse—

by Millow
above the
Bedfordshire
Levels—
opal blades
of sunlight
crown
ploughed loam
west to east.
Peewits implode
where tines
turn. Vast
music of
wood interiors.
He bags
chain-sawed
ivy vines.
With light
like this,
spilled
by deciduous
branches
and evergreen
leaves, the
copse
is a cathedral
of wild windows
and unexpected
doors. Why,
then, write
*wing sorrow
in strange light*?
Bagging-up
knuckles and fingers
of wood, hung
on handlebars,
listening the
fishless gully
whispers to Cambridge;
rodents rasp

in grass
on teazle banks—
he walks
the kindling
back to Millow
up the road
to a descending
sun.

•

As if—as
if one could
have humane perspective
and the sky
so black.
Where is she
now, anyway,
and what is
she doing?
Who does
she see?
Why am I
asking?
It is
foolish
to, more
difficult
than
pretty toes
and ruched sleeves.
Sea below
the gravestones
churns
and storms.
Thrift,
kale,
straighten
and bend.

Such light,
yet rage
in it, sleek
ignited.
Under
spasmodic
spastic
wing-flight
he stretches
every shattered limb—
aches
for a time
not sore.

•

In land
of beak
and claw
and fishing-line:
hush, love.
No moon
tonight—
where is it?
When prince
on wild laws
crushed
enemies most,
driving blades
deep through
their lives—
mayhem
in rowan
and heather.
Now it is all...
another tale
of the tribe.
Kes hangs
on tip
of a feast

dream, slow
whisper
of September
mornings; laugh
he might
if raptors
would. Soon
it's noon.
No, midnight.
Two or three.
Word merchants
not manicured
lurch
room to room
in unpleasant
disarray.
Get to know
what
the rodent knows:
clawed and riven
in a sike, on
moonless common
land, you die,
as beryl croziers
nod breezily.

•

Argent light
spills
through cordage
and plovers leap
light-winged
into a westerly
from hand-made
walls.
It is not
a sanguine time
and many shreds
lie dumped

in post-
industrial theme
parks ready
for a whinge.
The north is
a heritage centre.
Day-trippers,
weirdly ignited
by supplements
and just remembered
family lore,
flock to cram
the road edge—
taking home
in plastic bags
their leaded fruit.
O now
the sky
is jasper: badly-
bandaged gangrene,
so commonplace
as to be
an insult to
what you think
you know. At
mushy pooledge
several miles
below
his true stature,
Ranter—narked
and legless—
pores over
empty bottles,
polishes his
chanter—looks
towards
the world—
says nowt.

•

The report
said:

His conduits
blew. Craze
down the
wires, circuits
and loops—
melt-down.
Boards, grids
in final frazzle.
Razed earth
littered
five hundred yards
with rivets
and spoons.

He swayed
in the fire ring,
joints
popping sparks.

We foamed him
but what
he hadn't
head-banged
burned.

At 21:20
his last
solar-charged
transmitter
stopped saying
*her her her
her her
her*. The
crew cleaned
up, hosed
the area
down.

•

Wind-wild
in leg-soaking tussocks
he knew her best
as an enticing memory:
photographed
in a Bill and Ben hat
fetching springwater
in a zinc pail—sheep
at her backside
under bright rain.
Now she's a mother & mum.
Loves her
through seasons
of borage and rosehip,
light tumbling
through twigs and twines,
upturns and inclines,
tines turning
beneath the sun.

•

Tides clip these lands.

Gale in a copse
whips
bark-stockinged
trees.

Farne-
fussing, Farne-
fuming
surf, in
mighty
region
of kippers
and Bede.

He is
gone
from the whispering,
gone
to the long bar
for a strand
of comfort:
"Boulmer, continuous
slight rain."

Wild weather
between
us, again.

•

Blood raged high
for clart pants:
Cheviot chine
roped up,
fenced in.

Bales of wire
to be unrolled
and stapled
at hedgeless rim
by badly-paid men
down the dale.

Dreamed goring
them, butt those
betrayed him,
his turbulent
tribe. In
sikeslurry, snout
clogged, chanter
bust in another life,
one eye
on the world,
sniffing a late
windwhisper:

above dung
and heather,
brilliant borage sky
and starlight,
lawlip
above to
rosehip below—
such beauty
to quell
disgust
and shame.

•

Wind-pearled
webs dripping
rivermist:
hushed blades.
Pools turn,
say things.
A feathered
hunter
through the
copse—
vole's no
hiding place.

•

Would the wind—
on Knock Shield
tonight—between
roughing rosehip,
ask her to be
supple reminder
of stems not crushed,
pliant but hushed
footnote to greater works?
No, she is too wild.
Against domestic ruin

she clasped a shawl.
Yet she is upright
to earth, scornful
of gravity. Her
wandering is endless.

•

Such low
and brilliant
light

a needle
through
his heart.

Cleughs
and laws
go black.

The wind
is
dimmed.

The virtuous
drag
wings on Killhope

and beyond,
sup from
various pools.

But the light
has gone,
and it

gets
darker
and darker.

Ode

COMPLETELY FRAGGED IN THIS NEW DAWN
    with the stainless bint in No. 10
        a nation aches for harmony:
population culled Northumberland to Kent, as if
    a shrike at large
                beyond the normal row. Time
and small returns, bloodmoney on the road
   now the banner's down. Hotspur's done
his foolish marching
       and the pasture's cold, all traces
           rinsed to roots. Bede is with him
        in the sorry ground.

O many lost
        & harmful
                to a sudden core—

nothing
    like it
        under heaven.

Such confidence when the applause is blue!
      For we are harried from docks and mines
        to the very close, striking off
as best can. To fend too hard
      will dent your hands, dear one,
which I would not wish.

Now the complete ordinance
        weeps & moans
& the beautiful newsreader
        repeats each
tremendous fairytale.

from

Hellhound Memos

(1993)

[5]

Your tentship, your azureness, your cornflower
blue, flung over me, your right as rain, your
Bob's your uncle, please court my swelled heart.
Please spill me the dew from cusloppe's rim.
So much of life is weeping and stained
like broken spies, tables damp with distress,
the tea cold.
To frank a legend you say in Bodoni Bold: I
have boiled the earlies and now I can stand tall
in my yellow rape Jerusalem. Never believe it.
Prisoners in stripes, it was always so, nurses in white,
a marvel anyone lived.
Major minor not doing one thing about it.
And where, under this heaven, is my Mary?

[6]

Sky so very vast and blue. Puny we.
Lonnens ribbed against it.
Hellhound, thee with vast purchase, off, off!
my siren, my knocker, my foghorn, my bell.
Off my loose nails, my gate furniture, my slide
action latch, my epoxy-coated wire hasp, my B&Q
gate bolt, my free delivered catalogue.

So on a much-ignored and cloudy peak
in south Cambridge between the passing traffic
Several great men will undo their XL vests
And flex their special hinges.
One will not. He is alert in black corduroy.

Cut the chicken into large pieces.
Bring the milk to boil in a heavy pan.
If you have a heat diffuser
use it.
Puree the remaining flesh.
Chill until needed.

Sense the stars and the dark water.

Hellhound Rapefield Memo

Hellhounds horning in the rapefields.
Paranoid detectives in the crypt of St Mary Redcliffe.
August fourth fiends nosing the embers.
Me, I kick his sizzling heart around just as I like.
Devil in a pink shell-suit.
Anne Sexton, Robert Johnson, Barry MacSweeney at the crossroads
Swapping riffs on an Olympia portable, dreaming
golden waves of grain.
All alive on the 125, the 521, the 9, 10, 11, the
14, 15, 16, the who gives a toss, the extremely partial
statement train, the bogey Carmichael, the
estranged keyboard crew, the vast crucifixion industry, bejewelled
freedom for sows enbargement, flak directorship, all
of those plucking, strumming on the chuff-chuff Jesus train.

You could not hear them, you could not, hounds
slavering jawed
cat food down the porch into the fleeting shadow
of the orange blossom special,
the nostril flaring cocktail smell
of recently released cordite
of the obvious pharmaceutical interest
everyone will make money from now that there is a special,
not to say unique, clamour
above the hellhound kennels.

Filth it is a monument.
O lanceolate leaves the truth is yours!
A monument. Pink-suited hellhound over it.
I fear for my cusloppe, my betany, my bane, my cranesbill, my cuckoo
pinting gob of wayside spit.

The soapwort will best us all.

[12]

'The wild confusion dwells in me'.
: Christina Catherine Fraser-Tyler

for Arizona Dranes

So quiet tonight I can barely hear the brushing
of an angel's wings.
So quiet and pleasant it is as if I am in B&Q.
O Darlington Susan, what pleasant times
in the Calor Gas Centre at Scotch Corner before
we fled into the dales and yarns, the yearns,
the raw grass which greened our thighs and knees.
The sun was like a bucketful of gold!
The argent streams bubbled through our fingers and we hoorayed
with monumental whoops of elemental joy.
Like Wylam salmon male and female we whipped the Pennine bore.
We made a point of arguing. My shoes. Your shoes.
Your shoes. My shoes.
Whose dismal, scum-filled rain tonight is it anyway?
All claimants will come forward, Susan, wearing their darkest badge.

[14]

For Rachel Bierley

Rachel, darkness broods upon the temple tonight
and the account is almost to the bone.
The mallet's blow has once more hurled me down
and there are pawprints all over from ankle to craw.
Hounds swept through the gorseflowers fanging me righteous before
Robert Johnson could slick a nickel in the phone, before
Anne Sexton arrived at the pharmacist, before
Betty Blue obliterated all she could see, before
the arrival of the unlicensed gun.
It was a black and handsome .38.

Pink, pink, pink, you said, as I thought
of the Jesus Christ Almighty in white lawn
turning the tables and phlegming the fools.

Flashbulbs popped and blue lights circled
under sweet larch rain
and the head was at right angles to the spine
accordingly.

Garbled Manifest — No Hellhole Unturned

An absolute permutation of high-strung
misery threads the clouds today. Then the acid rain
comes down relentless, Bladerunner-style, breaching
levee and harbour wall. Groyne froths beneath its fall.

Right on time the devil's whore handmaidens rise tiptoe true
in white courts, bursting, roots showing from rhizome heads,
in furious lace and lawn, seeking Robert Johnson, Bob Dylan,
Anne Sexton and Barry MacSweeney. Those gnawing bitches

wearing ruby ankle-straps for pointless pleasure's
endless diversion at the Devil's Christroads, at
Dirt Pot at 23:59, sixty seconds before Year Zero, beck
running redundant lead ore waste and human blood.

Swapping Staffordshire pitbull and Rottweiler win
tokens, they swank delirious with gallons of snakebite
on what common ground's left, urine-stained madder and
harvest gold shell-suits, almost ready for an unwaged

basketball booted shoplifting forage into the mall, where
they'll meet popped tattooed dad, flung pissed out into
Gallowgate, who slurs: Stuck my finger right up the bus
inspector's nose, forecasting his immediate mortality

unless once more his inner breast pocket received that
leather-covered report book. It is true and all of this
you can convey in any lingo Sanskrit to Walloon,
tell St George under the phlegm-soaked Union Jack that

I have not being trying with much effervescence to overcome
my love for alcohol in favour of language lately.

[16]

> *'These days will be saturated
> with filth'* : Hildegard of Bingen.

Jerusalem has been sold and is a mall
with cross-Channel counter-culture accountants
selling rapefield hectares.
Instant zero-degree credit for the Chelsea sofa
and hand-painted Lake District bookends.

Struck livid with no purpose
beneath a choking sky, you want
Rachel and Aidan and Timothy
to do well and not have anyone
invade their little shoes.

Fleet golden light is sucked
into the rook wood midden and the closed pit. Once more
the hounds flow from rowan heather and gorse
fanging the moon to crescent cheese. They lap it up.
Charcoal presses its knuckles into the trees
and strangles the light away.

The judge, the brehon,
whipper-in from the fell and the law, the man
with ready index, the man with 'come on by' forever flirting
on his up-country utterance, the procurator
in his laminated two-piece and snowfall wig, he will descend
with an unforgiving rod and undying chain of command.

Die by myself with twin-feeder tubes.
Die by myself seven separate functions defunct at once
credit card blown burned to death in Consett
Tempest Vane Mercantile Dry Dock sometime lately.

[17]

> *'Silent is the house: all*
> *are laid asleep'* : Emily Brontë.

The malevolent honeyblack of the insect's
thorax and wings, brooding darkly
like cathedral windows tonight,
the ruby heart of the Jesus Christ Almighty.
Red and deep blood running at the Gallowgate crossroads
where Robert Johnson Anne Sexton Barry MacSweeney
hoy fury late chemist kitchen sink rota shrimp blues
onto the Olympia
as each accusatory index finger reaches its quarter to three
its nine fifteen
before the bairns Rachel Timothy Aidan know what's what what what.
How right you are to pant for air, adopt
a gutter to wash down your filth, seek a meeting
with complete freshness. It is great to be so well-pressed.

We gaze into the mauve sky-stitching.
Once more at Gallowgate beneath the blue star
under the black and white roar, the maniac milk.
When will we be shaved? When purged and cleansed?
Doctor, will the mite be foraged from our
speckled freckled skin? Will we sweetly sleep?

Can the knocking on your trapdoor
be ignored?

You can rely on it not ever being so.

from

Postcards from Hitler

(1998)

I am Lucifer

I am Lucifer

I am charcoaled prince of light, the ruler of the very sunne.
When I cough, with all of this fire, thunder leaves me.
Starres and security men, born to be welder apprentices at closed-down
                                                            shipyards
and shift-earners in devastated collieries from here to Vane Tempest,
                                                            England, UK,
where St Francis lived however temporarily in September, 1979,
and villages flee before my beautiful Italian 1966 blacksuede boots.
I look at the darkened beck and stones move.
Astronomers like Galileo looked to me for light.
Locksmiths wanting to accentuate the handling of guns
attempted appointments

But Pope Margaret said no

I go alone where no man goes
I am an Australian soap, I am tonsillitis in the bad end of Newcastle
and you don't want it.
There are too many Cambridges between you
and the love of your life

poetry

I am Lucifer

and I stare unbrokenhearted with my shredding scissors into the false
golden paper heart of heaven.
I am the main man, dressed in total French or Italian charcoal, guitar
sideways, no guitar, socks just right,
all busted heavens catching the blue bus

arriving at my fratchy scratchy well-oiled door.
Believe me, it's green, just like Sparty.

I am Lucifer

high pitch collar, no ties,
in some nowhere place, Devon for example,
cream teas, I am Lucifer,
no bonny white starched collar,
freak me, judge and judge and judgement mound, ye breakers
of bell-bottomed black-booted heavens,
go to your Tony Blair and Harriet Harman.

I am Lucifer,

the freak Jesus everyone wants to clean,
the bleak walker on the shore,
I am the car driver Desmond Davies,
the M11 crash victim,
the perfect stitch victim.
I am Lucifer, born on the southern-bound song-sound highway.
The Stevenage boy away for the game
on the red and cream bus.
I am Lucifer: Look at me!

Black wet suit, high heels, no shoes, tie made from eyelashes of moths.
There is a broken silver place for me,
there is no silver palace,
and it is not in heaven,
where Jesus lies upon his little frame.

I am Frederick Ferdingfang Lucifer,
          write poems at the age of seven.
I am who I am but no-one.
I am the kicked-over furniture,
the dragged by books,
the Percy Bysshe Shelley Shakespeare John Paul Chaucer postcards
sent from America, home like France and the great Russian, of beautiful
                                                        revolutions,

for there is nothing left remaining here in the United Labour Party States of England.

I am Lucifer,
little miss Froo Froo,
very Sixties white no-whats,
ah-ha, Marianne Faithfull,
Give it to you Neil boy, Tony boloney,
let's see what happens.

I am LUCIFER

the frank 40 seconds when we met in the desert
before female children were never speeded down
from the hills of Herod
before black Christians
adopted the aura
adapted the book

before they put put put on their walking boots and did up their laces
and their icicle feminist hearts

O rising world of waters dark and deep
listen you honeyboneys
put your aqua-ears to the earth I own
I am—I am—Lucifer

there is no-one above me and no-one below

Look how the words come upon me
and lessen my ends
they stand and stalk
it is all I can do to stand still
and not breathe flame
upon the universe
and all of the void poets
and their money bucket agents
who haunt the books

Stroke me, mildew crush, leaven my bones in the Pearl whitewater,
make my cock into a rattlesnake of ebony

I am apparently so brilliantly sincere, very tabloid,
just like Prime Mime Minister Blair,
but I am fulled with grievous deceit,

spiders rove my veins,
and Irish pipes.

then de Chirico
approached me
and wrote
a note
asking how to canvas
Spanish shadows

I returned his memo
sinned
and signed

yours eternally

yours venomously
without a mouser
that weepy brown thing
that failed 45

I signed it with blood and black ink

Yours damned forever

Mr Senor
All aboard the grief bus

Mr CromwellChartistTed Hughes SilvyPlath Gas Bill PayerJim Burns
                                                    Preston Spartak
Barry MacSweeney Moscow Dynamo Season Ticket holder
Yevgeny making your arrangements with the West
which were not Communists

Mr Rhythm in the night-class of night
I am—God Bless Him—

Mr Get Up Fancy a Cup of Tea Hello Pet In The Morning—

I will take every heaven in my stride
striding them down

Starres alone and only are glad of my darkness§§§§§§§§

Yours sincerely
altogether
mr absolutely
President not voted in yet

Totally all yours

and you only

Lucifer

I AM Lucifer,
I am beauchamp goat-on-her-behind Vivienne,
of Hammer Horror,
I am speaking non-person,
unspeakable daft wag.

waif in the windrow with a stolen version of Tommy Chatterton and
                                        Johnny Clare,
me the violent rudder victim.
Temperature-anus.

I am Bellevoire Beauregard,
Swing handy from the Noose,
believer in Next to Nothing,
Behaver of Badd Effects,
I start at the Dark End of the Street,
and I move, strange-wise:

They slanged my piece,
there is a darkblue mouse   or is it black
going all round my house
where was it born
and does it live on thrown-away clothes ready for the cancer shop and
                                        be kept warm by central heating
left on for days and nights
by the drunken devil who lives here
listening to Blind Willie Johnson [no T]
and reading everything post William Carlos Williams and Frank O'Hara
and Blind William Milton, just to hammer the message home, you braves,
including Ken,

when he's not
in the museum in Keld or Reeth

Lucifer?

Yesterday, February 6,
                    in the beautiful drenching rain,

after lunch in Alston and down from the wilderness,

with Anthony in a slate-silver Porsche,

Dirt Pot, near where Howard spun to death after a darts match,
just as it said in the Courant,

lights on but no U-bend control,
down to the wonderland of Dirt Pot
where the East Allen River is brazen with lead rime,

and the poetry of unsaddened youth

I've heard the sagging drawn-out withering whispers from putrid parents,

from the ice-cold well with its verdant tufted surrounds

to the muscular strokes through the water at the top of the tarn

and looking truly west,

the yellow Robson bulldozer, from Station Bank, Hexham, took away

the last of our Sparty cottage

and I hope God lies easy in his cream heaven

with his sufferance

of Urthely

man and woman-made pride and vanity

because my heaven was stolen from me

My Lucifer's dancing delight

Hello, love,

my spring larkin,

my understated cannykin,

vast heroine,

fullmouthed gobpersonne,

I sung of Chaos and eternal Night,

I've only just understood,

What Milton wrote in his coming darkness,

what he said turned down by Oliver,

what he wrote when he could no longer fascinate himself upon the
                                                                        verdant meadows

of brilliant England, when it was brilliant and not a home

to pink-suited mental geriatrics on the make

all dressed in black, with white collar:

O my Pearly goodness!

Light and greenness will always be a light to me,

Those before us—

and only those—

betrayed us.

Yours with very everlasting love

Bar Mahooley Kooney MacLooney

In the true John Wayne country I ask where God—that spurious socialist—

is supposed to be

I abuse everything in this pitiful landscape
blackened with industrial disease
finished and copped
fratched and begging on its knees and hands for money
crawling the A-roads
fantastic and unloved

There is a sirtainty
A given calm
which no government has used recently
not since Milton anyway
or use of language
I will never imprison lies
or colours or the lives of wonderful painters
or poets

There are many principles and principals and Parliamentarians and
                                                                     Prime Ministers
but not one so fantastically great
and with such lascivious bystanders
or attachers to Cyprus and sinne

and there are billions of principles
no matter how you spell it
all the way from Leamington Spa
and all of those who worked hard against me
spat upon it
but I ride a wide-looking and wild charcoal horse
not like the bank
and I feather the perry's air, close to the earth   Jesus said was his
And I leaf the aire
green as modern bark
and my charcoal bonny love speaks flame, as we ride through the low
                                                                      heavens,
above Kielder and Nenthead,
wanting to get the consonants and vowels,
and pay the correct cash at the post office—still under the customage
of Her Royal Majesty I see—

There are only the wild speeds of mad drugs and night—

And Shelley

to whom I handed over this horse

and he wanted to know if it was a vegetarian
or Ted Hughes

There are parts, coal buckets, becks with brown trout blinded with lead usage,
and there are parts of this whole universe to which my black wings have not
fathomed.

When the sun sank, I did my forkedfeet in and laughed harder than Alston
lunchtime chips.
I looked the colour black right in the face and stared it right down.

There was a colour about it, not from here, it must have been Sunderland,
a weird football team of which I have never heard except when planets
explain their past doings.

There are parts, ports, places and they **are** black, like my spirit and soul

Do I ever cease my wandering
in search of sacred song?

Since the Pavilion Hall, Buxton, April 27th to 30th, 1976, we sprayed
around our heat,
we daily broke the mould.
There was a skull you held and displayed and you got it from the general
and we were magnificent with it like Hamlet.

So much the rather you, in the holy light
ascending up and across the rim of the law,

O my dear Barry, give me all of your love, with all of the politics, and no
                                                                  man-given God,
stop the whistling train when it goes through Pecos without stopping
                                                 and whistling three times

O my dearest Lucifer, darling devil of the coal-fire eyes
in sulky shining silk
when you kiss me goodnight
all of my little ridges
expand and nudge the heavens

O my baked breadbun
O my dearest darling Barlamb
O my fast-mouth freak late-train leaver
O my croissant fetcher before I've even bathed
and warmed to your brilliant dewdrop breast kisses
O my horrid stamping Lucifer nuisance
O my man who doesn't know the birthdays of godchildren
My weepy Bar
when Newcastle lost Andy Cole and Kevin Keegan left
and Alan Shearer was injured for almost the whole season
O my brilliant poet

Beatitude beyond utterance

O my Milton my Shakespeare my Shelley
but not all of the same things in one day whenever you're sober, dear one,
you Bruce Willis fan,
dispenser of darkness,
vast wilderness explorer in the up a height and wildly raining,
my broken shoulder-bladed fierce fall-down-the stairs bonny bairn.
My warrior for justice and light.
My sable snake, my ebony Adam of the jet skies,
Driving unalone by starrelight,

My Lucifer.
My love.

February-April 1998
Newcastle

My Former Darling Country Wrong or Wrong

The desperate hypocrisy which bleaks every day my long-held belief in life
and its future and its hope has vanished and is gone like the shipyards I knew

and the collieries where I looked on pit-heads as if they were cathedrals
standing above the horizons before they were managed to Hell by Arthur
                                                                                              and Margaret

My life has not been long in terms of universal experience
but sometimes—often, even—I lie upon the strangely-cheap carpet

foaming into my Irish brew, and gag, and freak, and finish inside the hospital
at the inability of almost everyone I know—especially so-called revolutionary
                                                                                                                  poets

with their passes into the circus of brilliant new hard-nosed books as if Melville
and William Burroughs and my dear dad's Charlie Dickens had never existed

or Dostoevsky's The Idiot had never hit the now completely forbidden streets
where we step right over the glue and flung bad chips and curry sauce and
                                                                                                             puke up later

God knows—and there is one, you know—and he is called Milton and Blake
and Litherland and Silkin and he and she, one person combined, is called
                                                                                                                 somewhere

under each of our own heavens, is Dusty Springfield and Carl Wilson and
                                                                                          William Shakespeare
and he or she walks the very brilliant night under the rain of our land so
                                                                                             putly-wrong

We defy sequence, not understanding what comes down the ripped-up
                                                                                            railway before us
It is nothing, it is a laugh, it is what we might think about for one second
                                                                                                   perhaps

before the arrival of Colin Sandwich from quite another planet we might know
My country, tramp and tramp no more, my country wrong and wrong and
                                                                wrong into the darkness

my poor nation, my country brought to the once brilliant knees which held
                                                                           Cromwell
in a sway and spray of meadowflowers which delighted all of England except
                                                               where where Royalists

where Milton, in eternal blindness, dictated Paradise Lost to his daughter
in the same arena of the universe—we were starres apart—where Pearl
                                                                            learned to read

Her little pencils and crayons are a mighty thought to me these violent
                                                                          saddened days
and blindness and deafness and the lack of memory slowly creep upon me
                                                                          caused by disuse

and even though literate and able to write voluminous sentences as long as
                                                                     the River Allen East
there is no wisdom in what I say especially on the rug in the front room at
                                                                        two in the morning

I long for the cry of all of the wild birds I know upon the wind between the
                                                                        wires which work
from the funny little paths which descend from Burnhope Reservoir to Carr
                                                                           Shield down

O my love, my nation, o my birthplace of everything from John Bunyan
                                                                      to Johnny Rotten
I love you so much your ICI-polluted light and your cleared smoking
                                                                    chimneys gone and gone

There is a burning feast of buttered bitterness upon our tongues this
                                                                    after-chapel Sunday
There is a dinner on our slavering wronged and wine-soaked tongues begging
                                                                   for Brit UK meat
Preferably right on the bone

II

Flit the Jesus Christ Almighty orange juice from the roundabout supermarket
                                                               with petrol station and
plenty of parking, I don't want any of that milk for me or my family

At aged seven only sent to the byre I was happy as a pig in clarts to tweak
                                                                    the tits until the bubbling
snow went into the pale
long before Tolstoy swept onto my fjord-gazing eyes and then Lenin and
                                                                               Mayakovsky
and Yevtushenko and Ginsberg swept away the almond-shaped eyes of people
                                                                            I had never seen
before

III

I have been there, several thousand times, and don't want to know
I Lucifer am flying with God-kissed charcoal blackened wings
away from a country I no longer wish to fear and know

My God other than me
you are so far from Carr Shield
you are in Cowshill
and you do not know me

Portering the world is a steady business, and you need unshaking hands
                                                                               and clear vision
fired with astounding passion which everyday reaches the skies, and the
                                                                               gorgeous starres

is what poets must and always do

I woke this morning to the broken laced-down light
which moves in such dramatic fashioned grace

all of the way from Coalcleugh down the great rivers
towards the working mooring berths of the offshore fields

O my nation, my uninspired telephone connection, my inability
to buy the collected poetic works of George Barker and Francis Thomson

The frequency and zenith of betrayals has almost left me frantically agape
and riveted to a million wild points and profits of unwelded behaviour

So I will escape you my wondrous Valhalla

my poetic headland beaming like a leadminer's lamp bobbing and weaving
                                                    in the spring darkness

the helicopter gunships are fanning the landing strips and the dust is rising
the beautiful English moon is high and we wait for the sunne and everything else

is silence evermore

March 1998

Horses in Boiling Blood

(1997-99)

War Roses

poem LXXVI — Poèmes à Lou, Apollinaire, p.230

Such amazing fireworks light over steel
Total forked lightning beautiful and true
Madfire murderers   Madmen flamebearers
Smiling with courage you periscope the enemy

Two Himalayan roses brilliantly exploding
Expanding like breasts their very best bra-hooks
Stretching out bedroom-darkened fingertips
They must love to tell the German sky   They're dead now

A poet inside Kielder Forest
Stands flinty and aloof from the pain
His French Army issue revolver on safety
Some roses of this war die in complete silence

Roses abandoned dying and dying: comrades
He will strap his gob upon the cool park fountain
Beside the runback path through the escape trees
I walked there every night—fast—like Oscar Wilde

The roses—my men—bleed like subjects from the rimdom
of the Marquis de Sade—and suddenly his head bends over—
a beautiful red rose reduced and reduced by Bosche brutality
Spreadeagled like your bedroom-lit softly curved haunch-hips

The air is crammed with completely mad spirits
Sieved through the light of newly-discovered stars
Howitzers weep above us in their sudden flight
Death, shattered petals, loving death to France's finest

*

Every single promise of love is well below you
And who will put your signature on the world as a poet
O rose forever fresh despite bombardments   O ready rose
Instead of beauty I offer disgusting perfume of death and blood

You flowers who will not give up your medals when surrendering
O permanent combat soldiers the dawn gusts have mistreated you
Flowers soldiers combat conscripts filled with hope of victory
They are wrapped up linament thank Christ no more bleeding

They cry as I approach them
I am only trepanned and have lost no limbs
The Pearlmoon is so tender
We flow backwards into our tidal gutterage & filth

It is as fatal as a great Northumbrian piper who will not listen

I balance my future air on the crystal of clouds
My badness at once will vanish from me despite this terrible war

And clouds will now very soon claim and clam down upon us
dark & unforgiving   forever

July 1998

Troubled Are These Times

Cushy days have gone forever
    from marigold beds   to a land called Hell
My ring blue but the mind is oppressed and black
    Cushy days heaven on earth crushed and gone
Cowboy bootlace ties snapped and hoyed
    Mist around the Tour Eiffel has turned to fog
I am no longer up to my thighs in trench-water
    I am up to my Adam's apple in the dreaded gargle
O Esmerelda   Drive that taxi drive that cab
    Keep this broken poet & brother off the cold cold slab
We want a future   We want to see the herbs
    Re-seed for at least eight million years
It is almost winter and we want to see
    Northumbrian snow sleeving the beautiful boughs
It will be like wedding dresses right through the forest
    Words that spring to mind will be **bridal** and **virgin**
And the only **darkness** will be layered like silk
    On the little wings of the snow bunting not yet left
The Kielder Ride potholed in the way we love
    Paris only two train trips away   One under the sea
6:10am exactly but darke this September dawn
    Darke and darke from one soul to another
Fame will come upon us but for most different reasons
    We shall be found in the night stretched and strung
Unless protected against the endless harm of the world
    Harmlessness such a precious condition these days
Rage will seek and find its squadrons of permanent ire
    And there will be nothing left but night night night
And within the night there will be night night night
    The heartbroken however will seek & find their true station
Esmerelda drive that yellow taxi through the pouring rain
    There is no tomorrow and the snow bunting has flown
There is no tomorrow and all swannes have deserted the Elvet
    There is no outlook and the dashing sky-high swifts
Have abandoned the large and lowering cloud formations
    Darling o Darling there is no tomorrow only coffins

It used to be pelting rain but now it is tears pouring down
    There is dawn sunshine dearest but heart cleavage is royal
And at the bitter corrosive forefront of all of our sad duration
    Darling our axles poles rods shafts spindles
Our chassis
Is broken destitute and completely penniless
these awful days
    I am the original Elvet swanne with blanch wings
I swanned alone in the wreckage of riverweeds waiting for Thee
    All I ate was a destitute menu of brook sludge
Waiting to twin and twine my snowy nuzzle and hugneck

The world gonne mad Mrs Goebbels poisons her six children
    They belong to Hitler and so they must die
No amount of sky as paper No amount of clouds No amount
    of sea as ink can spell out the terrible awesome tragedy
It's the thinness of the limbs and skulls and the six-pointed starre
    Which tears apart and breaks your so-called civilized hearte
May the eighth May the eight May the eighth May the eighth
    Returning to the walking position if possible the children
Experimented upon with injections by Dr Mengele & amputations

I have exchanged my beloved stone walls for sinks and sickness
    For the longing lutes of sadness which drive mad my brain
All the crosses on the graves demand reason for conflict
    And the ire will ascend like fire and torch our minds
It will scorch us for not importing the guillotine
    and not executing enough members of the royalty

Treachery and dumb appointments stalk the mad earthe
    We try and avoid their cunning devious shadows
So they do not fall upon our Cuban-heeled biker boots
    And sully our already badly-riddled heartes & soules

A singular circlet of amateur arrangements has harassed
    My neck all day worse than German gunnes
This was a peak of underachievement at its berry vest
    It is an icon of Gerry the Boche at his very best

There is that moment when the gunnes start and you think
   I should have written another postcard to Jacqueline
And several other treasured people you love admire and need
To make sure the corpse gets home and is destroyed with dignity

      As a mark of respect
      We are closing France
      My wonderful France
      We are shutting it down
      It isn't far in the Larousse

            From Guillaume
        To Guillotine

Four million will stand in the trenches and watch the one coffin
There will be postcards from loved ones tomorrow and the cafés
Will be locked and bolted against the invasion of terrible death
We have received all betrayals now and I want to hear from Pablo

I want to kiss the black saddle & the bicycle steel horns of the bull
There are thousands of Joan Miró sunnes and they Will rise again
But there are no postcards from Dusty   They are suspended
Because of the great beauty of the nation I respect grieve for & love

O Paris my dearest when will I see Thee again
    My Milky Way my cobblestones My brilliant cafés
I will not even catch the Metro from Gare de Lyon
    I will walk up the Rue St Denis to the Agile Rabbit

Mmm   Who are you in the white silk stockings Ah Madeleine
    When a German Howitzer shell crashes into your face
Just before your head comes off Your inner tongue
Spouts it out: To whom shall your officers send the telegrams

I stand here thigh-high in muddy water blitzed by shelles
& quite frankly I don't care who are the lieutenants of the future
And you talk to me about refutation and difficult positions
    Nor will I talk about it   Leave   I'm sending shells which explode

Green leaves are turning to brown especially in the crater holes
    Where with the cordite upon them they have been awarded
No natural end to their lives on the tips of the trees
    They are like my comrades   Burned to eternal life i.e. Death

Their boots are now a funny shape lying in the mudde
            And their heads even stranger no eyes and noses
I saw one of my sergeants with seven fingers
    When I had coffee with him this morning he had ten
And two thumbs   One of which he used to cock a rifle

To split the hearts and skulls of those grey-suited primitives
who are trying to rape and overtake my gorgeous republic
They will not they will not those from the land of Bavarian cakes
I am from the republic of croissants and we shall repel them

O dear Napoleon you kissed the big flag and just like Thee
    I am France and France is me
Catching my left index finger pushing through the mud
    A broken-down gun-carriage I could barely write this poem

But what do you expect the waves were like those at Bordeaux
            And on the salt marshes and in Marseilles
When the tide comes in with the sardine fishing-boats
    I long for them and my heart is like an unplucked harpe

My tongue has not yet flicked along the holes of a harmonica
    I don't want gunnes I want Bob Dylan and Emmylou Harris
I want time to write a poem swifter than a snipe drumming
    Even the telephone here in the trench is not as sweet
as the cry of my beloved peewit as it skims the upland earthe

The radio telephone is monstrous and not bird beautiful
    Its messages when we lift the receiver suggest we may die today
It freezes your eyes and makes your heart so cold
    You dream of the young lass in the cous-cous café in Berbes

And you swaggered in   In your new motorbike jacket
             And the biker's obligatory white silk scarf
But she drew her burnt gold curtains against your fantastic
         Revving and against your fierce glare of pure magnetism

Yet I know here that we shall begin again in times of freedom
         When war has stopped its terrible intervention
And your little pair of dollypops high-heels are by the window
     Now we rue the very streets but soon we will be liberated

The diamond and other gem starres shine in the heavens
     Despite all the bullets which whizz above our heads
Mars ascends so scarlet shaming the other planets for brightness
     Except the moon which I singularly compare to Paris

It is a tangerine in a flood of aubergines
It is the light of my life
It is a candle lit when the darkest hour has come
It is
The truth

Inspired by Guillaume Apollinaire
Septre 6e 97

Feast of Fashion Burning Down: Zone

Man among heart-thieves, endless disputes
man alone with 40,000 others
in a starre-system of their own
    where the aeroplanes go
we flew apart at the end of the old world
we flew together and then apart in a feast of moons and heifers
oddly-coutured harlequins beneath a high harvest
when you are dreaming of Pearl
and it is too long drinking & dreaming
newspapers every day and their manifold police stories

<u>shock</u>
<u>horror</u>
<u>Probe</u>

meanwhile the Germans are bombing us as if no tomorrow—which there isn't
the new cars are invading the streets of Paris   forgive our gaz
On the other hand, don't We are modernists
I am spit on the pavement

I have your tears and tears on the telephone
I saw this morning a beautiful street whose name I don't remember
it was Northumberland Street, Newcastle-upon-Tyne
A city I have never been to and do not remember

I went once to Hexham and stamped my little feet
They looked at me sideways
I stood at the war memorial
not knowing that my dad had fought in the trenches
before he left us and never spent any time teaching me the ABC
like you did

And he never loved you as you should have been loved as I loved you
As I plucked
                    a marigold

before you said Mayakovsky
Esenin
and I
bloody boy Chatterton Shelley Shakespeare and Blake

WHAT WAS THAT **FIRST** WORD

R
    a
i
n

it was filled with women of unusual hue and fantastic attraction
every day that passes a siren goes   not any more! Swans dead

Everything clamours: the big signs, the big men, the darling secretaries
all the way from Monday to Saturday—and now, of course, Sunday!
This is what I said to the day: you fuck, you fuck, [Pacino] you German
aeroplanes. But how the skies are so exquisitely gorgeous and filled with
peachen light.

The entire universe is jacks and planes and locks and doors
and abstract ideas in which there will be plenty of time to remember.

Adios America apparently so the voyages in my head are just too far

The voyages of the clouds are such beauty I never want to be attacked in the
mud. The aeroplanes can hammer us but we will not die.

I am a poet and a fighter not a Pope

                                            you don't know the intricacies and
lunacies of the cathedrals and love

here is the young street
the one of blue and white
it's nine o'clock the petrol has gone from the tanks

and now you're asleep with someone else
while we die in the trenches

All the flies fly by

and the tremendous resurgence of the troops has ended
thank goodness

You pray all of the night in the wings and shadows of the
Dartington college in Devon with the American deconstruction mistress
to where you have not visited and sniffed cocaine

There is an amethyst profundity in the whole of the universe
which will never turn to the eternal glory of the Jesus Christ Almighty ever
We always aim towards the eternal beautiful
it is the beautiful blue and dark blue lilies
which we used to cultivate

I have a million reasons for bringing them to you, savage, every one,
a man alone, without future, it is nothing and I have nothing to lose

They are the most glorious and magnificent lilies we have ever grown
It's the torch in the red hair that will not be extinguished by the wild wind
Never turn to the flamboyant glory of Jesus
That's the pale boy and painfully distressed mother
Forever it will be a fully-flushed tree beneath my praying palms
I am nowhere but in a trench miles away from Grey's Monument
That's the double gallows of honour and eternity

It's the starre of six branches of the night attack

It's the so-called God who dies on Monday and rises again on Saturday
It's Jesus the most sanctimonious man on TV and
It's not his fault
He's wearing a beard but he's not called Jesus he's called JeremyBeadle

Situated at Grey's Monument between Northumberland Street and the
children of the next universe

as in verse
It's Jesus who soars to the heavens higher than the aviators
He prevents everyone getting to the heights and sitting beside him

It's called death in the trenches beneath the aeroplanes
Pupilchild Jesus Christ Almighty of the eye on the world
the Pharisees and Germans came they were not even Nazis by then
there were no flashes no lightning strikes no Vingtième pupille
des siècles il sait y faire

It will all change when the bird dies and flows upwards towards Jesus
into the beautiful air

The demons in the rising gaping caverns know what to do
Elbow don't start rattling those bones around!
The demons raise your head above the parapet and then you
become a blonde with a head ready to be popped off by a German

The shadows say you are Judas and imitating Simon of the Desert
They chase you and try and catch after you in the street calling you a
thief: You fool! They say HE's The Thief! Icarus Enoch of
Birmingham Ely of Dublin Bobby Sands you madman Apollinaire

I only wanted to get up to urinate and say against the stark dawn light:
the fist comes out of the web of clothing like a leg of lamb

But it has no rosemary

Big poet man in the first-ever aeroplane—don't you deny me! I can see
you from here in les tranches
St Exupéry, climb down!
Those prayers which arrive eternally upwards towards the host

Freakjob, handjob, kissjob, explosivemind subject,

The ibis on fire   the crags of the maribou crane

Zero human, nowhere person, lost in the rain in New York
I do not want to keep a straight face   You're a T-shirt
you're a gunne a fathom job so long helicopter pilotesse
you're a helicopter gunship you're a fucking rave maniac

It's the wrong time the incorrect place the inconvenient moment
That's the zebra hour it's the place of the ibis the squarm of the stalk
It's the palace, the Utopia, Zion, the home of God, the quack of the duckwalk

Savage childe, remember your endlessly mindless place

Senior matrons boss me and don't believe me that I was in an endless
aerodrome I was I was A French poet killed in World War One
I wore a Bowler Hat what will you do Give Me A Medal?
dorsiflexion comes upon us   we arrive at the badly moment time

bonetime is a thing of the living world and not for thee
and hopefully not for me here in the grave trenches I wish
gapeful we stretch into the daylight trying our best to believe
and seeking breakfasts we search and search looking for succulence

O golden eagle

Let me wear my white stockings and my high-heeled high-strapped
cobbledehoys and sit upon you until we both come and let the Germans
die

When I'm worn out myself I will tear the Zeppelins from the sky
unroll my stockings and curl my feet against yours like gondolas

THE SKY IS EMPTIED now OF MILLIONS OF SWALLOWS

the angels flit about authorized by the happy flitter

the eagle from the air disturbs the hiboux

then is the immaculate voice of the spirit of columbine

and the swerving sky-ridden peacocks brought in the encyclopedia bought
by Susan

The next minute you're a pile of passionate ashes

Here we are in the perilous straits and confines
The sirens of death are appealing to the ends of the earth
The calls of the guns are arriving three by three
They are such friendly and familiar violent machines

Now you walk in Paris completely alone through the throng
The busflocks lowing in the avenues and boulevards rolling by

The phoenix butcher will be reborn again
the very moment that you are reduced to filth and furnace-endings
thinking you'll never live
You Lazarus driven insane by sunlight you bastard
You German twats
You men with machine-guns
You murderers of the French
You stupid invaders

Corstopitum cor petal
the Romans have gone and Aislinn
to London and Geneva
I am bereft of sense
but I can reach her on the mobile

087 564248

don't torment yourself with the open address book to Dublin

you'll fall in the Forty Foot you'll jump in the Murphy's before the

Germans come
You'll die of a bombed out bowler hat

You'll fleece yourself you'll
you'll do that you'll
There is no shameful disease there is no question there is Nothing
There is Zone Zero
There are only big guns   It is a complete nightmare   A voice in the
darkness Forgive me Lord I am in a trench   It is Nothing

It is only with my Strength and everyone else's
that we save the world from the Great Beast

My light dying it is forever daylight except at night

Farewell
The sun is chopped off by its neck
The sun is strangled
And so are my comrades

Autumn 1997
Inspired by Apollinaire
from ZONE

Terrible Changes

A woman bleats & cries in the night She has lost her bloke
        Howay pet O howay our lass
Just because you've lost your fella   The lads are marching back from hospital
towards the Germans
          O howay honey I'll take you doon the Bigg Market
Wear your clip-clops and groovy stockings

I'll take you out in white courts from Next doon the Toon
    First Bourgognes   Then the Duke   We'll stagger down Dean Street
            and celebrate our great victory of love over darkness
O Killhope Wheel by the recovery farmhouse where the medics wait for work
      flaying the untickled brown trout from the burn
There's nowt we can do about it flower   The wheel must crush lead

      Howay man pet we'll go to the Fujiyama for sushi and beef
        Come on honeybunch I'll buy you a new bra in Fenwick's
I'll buy it while you drift elegantly to the food department to buy the Napoli Salami
      The Fenwick's deli is the best in town
Our trenches were lit up by the brightness of shells destroying real men
        Can you imagine only one arm at the age of 24

Hey Pizzaland! Here we go!
I've seen the shells open the skie like petals and blow legs off
Petlamb divvent worry   It's the Quayside for us
Tuxedo Royale

You fear everything has altered
In my heart
But nowt has
I'm your crazed lover
EVERYTHING
My love is saved forever
Turks Head Here We Come!!

after Apollinaire
Septre 97 Just before the Hellbound Trail Tour

Ode to Snowe

after Apollinaire's L'avenir

I cannot wait for the froste to come
It will harden the sprouts and cool my ardent heart
But like the vegetables it will harden my sapper's sap
And make my heart truer to you than it has Ever been

Roll the bales of hay for winter
The farms will need them when war is done
Write your letters to dear ones
And stand to attention when told to

Let us smoke a pipe at nightfall
And dream of recovering love
The lieutenants are all around us
But enjoy the trench dogroses

The torrent of shells upon us never fails
The sky still gold And the hay good for the cannon horses
Just look at the bee
And don't think of the future

Look at our hands firing the artillery
They are as white as snow with the cold and rain
The dogroses running wild and the bee
And the future   I shrug   is also vicious and violent and untamed

Août 97

Victory Over Darkness & The Sunne

after Apollinaire
and in memory of Tatlin and Esenin
Mayakovsky and Malevich

Grouse bark in the heatherholes and the whitebeams
play musick like Corelli and Handel by the East Allen River
Their leaves sound in the night like the pleas of poor seamen
On the Herald of Free Enterprise upon its stricken side

Its hull balances swivelled into the sea and turned like Icarus
Turning from a god of travel to nothing more than a midge
The puddles reflect us as we walk and walk towards death

We smile a lot however drunk on the finest Bordeaux and Chianti

My diamond shining heart which will speak and speak forever
You're three hundred miles away now and I miss you and miss you
My lamps around the little house and my pierced helmet

Just look at the beautiful stone-cutting in Dean Street and Grainger
Street not to mention St Cloud and Sacré Coeur
                        The days were pure as beryl gems

The whole war from the trenches was like a firework display
The shells hung in the air like roses and other flowers
Fetching blood and light and other stranger beings

        You became scared of the sky
like a bout of unstoppable hiccups

You thought at night about the difficulties
Because our success depended on fellow people being dumb and stupid
Officers for example
                        There is a new language to learn at war
Youngsters have to be prepared to die at will

When the academics stay at home like 1968 and have nowt to say
When their minting of coinage is stooped in a university study

The language needed a blood transfusion and was near death
It lacked life and was beaten to fear and death by several poets
They did not do any good to poetry and were not there when it mattered

Did you notice how they weren't on the ferry to Paris in 1968?
They're just a bunch of silent film starres

     But if we work tough enough
     the language will be kept alive
   And the mutants & enemies will be driven down

We want new sounds not neat Faber and Faber
we want new sounds no Simon Armitage
with hands in the pockets of his suit in Paris
half a pound of badly-fried chips on each shoulder

I say: Fight the language which is nailed and then driven down!
To let it go is a sign of complete lack of civilization
But reclaiming it my dearest poets
       is a tremendous prize

Our Katie gives me two daisies picked from Whitbeck Road
    making more noise of the heart than what we say
Saying she loves me and I kiss her lip better   Twice
     Farewell memories of the past Pure nostalgia
Nobody likes the nomadic nature of love
When you hope for new & beautiful women to come into your life
O my dear darling dollbird hurry home
As soon as the Great North Eastern Railway will bring thee
    And
Look at the way I look at you with a clearer eye

These hopeless railway companies are making me yodel with sadness
They are ridiculous but trains are always beautiful
In the pouring rain on Platform 2 the 2 lights of the 225 shine in the mist
Reminding me of the fantastic shine of your grin in the rain
I bow over like a wedding ceremony to kiss you And your freshly-trimmed
hair   You great beauty
And I am miserable that we aren't together even though like Elvis sang

      I wear your lapis and silver ring
Our laughter even when we talk on the telephone spreads like butter

All around the house and the very world

Let's speak with our hands and clap them together in a high-five
Let's strike them like a gypsy tambourine   Wild and famous
                          O you wildwind words
          She walks through the berried rowan
            Love and no love walk around crying out their eyes
I am the sky over Greys Monument
I am the sky beyond the Haymarket and beyond that

         Listen to the roaring tide at Craster and the Farnes

Listen to the moaning tide faraway at Dunbar singular and lonely
            My faithful voice in the darkness of Denton Burn
            You think you are the last clear voice on earthe
The tidal causeway at Lindisfarne can be as untrue as you
            Just as Basil taught me all of those years ago
And he said if you don't publish correctly the tidal charts
Seamen from Valparaíso and Houston will end up on the Black Middens
dead on the rocks

Their cries echoing under the tidal sweep like the organs
of St Nicholas and St Mary's in the hearte of the city
And like St Denise in the outskirts of beloved Paris
And when the sun rises from the fjord's darkness
will only be in their death if you do not correct your tidal charts
Accuracy is all he said and also compression of language

Words are all we cannot live without   They tremble in the night
You should say to your hands please do not forget me
I love both of you at the typewriter and also at Persian prayer

What a relief it will be   a real Fenwick's window to hug you
You know   There will be many new things to do   Now we're not at warre

O my tongue slurs but I wish to lap the shore of life
and sound like Kerouac's Big Sur

And from St Malo to Craster and Seahouses
I speak the beautiful language of the Northumbrian waves

Sometimes I convulse and fit and my hands sleep in the street
until children find me and call the paramedics

Yet my fingers like me are face down in the heart of the city
My eyelids broken and lips bleeding I stagger home   Streets dead
Longing for the sharp winds of my homelands

As dead as the rail company which has cancelled all trains after 10.40pm
Look   Listen

Victory over all enemies is before us
Including addiction
Look towards the future
Look towards everything you can see
Or your dearest loved ones

And give your life a new name

Oui!

Alors finis
C'est tout
Août 24

Cornflower

    Young poet Barry
    only 20
    Already you have witnessed the appalling world
    What is your judgement on the adults who betrayed you

You   You
    faced
        death
            on the   learned ways of cheating
                    beautiful
                           Moto Guzzi
                               Californian
                                 drunk
                                    1,000 times

You told Elaine

    You were a brave nightrider

        And crashed
smashing yo   ur knees
On the A20   Then the M20 as if they named if after You
       handsome bridegroom
Filled with endless happiness
And covered in the blood of a wedding

        My heart a huge Soviet flag

            Ray Davidson and Mark Hyatt had already died by their
own hands   Wilful and deranged
   Despite the efforts of me with Ray   I spat Ray   She isn't worth it
He would not take off his Mod glasses and would not listen at the Big
Lamp

and Jeremy and me on the nightride to Manchester
        One with chloroform and one with pothole pills
In that order

        At 5pm you rang and said goodbye   My bride
         And I drank myself to death   Twice   Three times   Four

I learned nothing from my so-called betters
    But I am a sterner Miltonic man
        I stared death in the face
            but not life
        O darling times in the various Kentucky and Tennessee
blue grasses
          We're at the stupid red lights now

Août 97
After Apollinaire

Cold Mountain Ode

I am Cold Mountain and Wolf on the Treeline
I am fargone on a galleon and an oil-seeping tanker
I have travelled all of the way to the Orient and still never been there
There is no truth in Beauty Keats was error-ridden

Yet still I give it all the world's credence with a capital consonant
There are 365 days in one year and I have seen all of them 49 times
Why should I Be Lonely sings Aaron in one of Jimmie's best songs
I am Cold Mountain the wolfish monk who stalks the top of the lawrim

I speak to the wild geese in the garden and know them better than Thee
I lie flat on my stupid back and watch the Arctic terns and know them better
Than thee than thee than thee than thee than thee denier of my hearte
I travelled with Prynne though the Kielder Ride and we spoke

Of the abstract beauty of the planted larches and firs
And amazingly spotted in the pathway a snow bunting
And when we rode up to the Scot border Prynne said Wyoming
And for once in my life I knew it was absolutely veritable and true

And I knew that one day in the future with monk's paw I would write it down
The sleeve of the habit on the right arm would have to be retrieved
And that the eternal hood of the man in black would have to be demolished
And that the buttons would have to be sewn back onto your suits
Because you were never meant to be a Mennonite or Amish but always a Mod
And black suits are in man skybluesocks and handmade Cheaneys or
Grensons   White socks are passé so very James Dean frownwise
And when the grain tumbles into the silos you will need a hat
Today midnight the first Harvest moone of the year bronze coin
And Guillaume drops in another postcard saying he'll be back
Despite the trepanning and his expected long stay in hospital
Before being transported with the rest of the lads back to shoot at Germans
O World your beauty is a crazed expression I see it every day but can't believe
Men with one hand and half an arm hauled back to the Front appalling
They should have been sent home to the vingtième arrondissement
The twentieth the only Communist one remaining in Paris and selling chard

They should have been delivered back to their homes near the Bastille
To the home of the tricolor and the settlements of the black flag
From the waisthigh water and the stars of the wilful shrapnel
Every man had a poem under his helmet and there was no tomorrow
Good Lord what IS going on in this place Bill Dead   Allen gone   Is Ed dead
I wake up at last and get the news It happens And I drink 230 pints of wine
And I see you and we agree some kind of arrangement which is right by me
And right by you and on your glasses go like a protection against Barglare
Split infinitives are a special portion of my nature just lately
Especially when berated at the crossroads between Ashleigh Road and The
Drive by your so-called mother and being branded evil in front of neighbours
At nine-thirty in the morning as if a complete criminal I am drunk but deny it
Not a criminal but a human being with every effort to shake off the chains

After Gwill and Snyder and unfinished—so far Août 9

Sam Arrives to Take Grandad for the Dawn Tickling

I always envied it and thought he was well handsome
My Grandad with his grey spike hair often touched with engine oil
Our Calvert past is so tremendously noble and on the edge of a cliffe

It wasn't magic you know us kids kneeled there trying to learn
We sat next to Grandad thinking the whole world was in his pockets
And it was   with lorry spanner and intricate penknives

Staggering back in the absolute night from the Allenheads Inn
With a stop-off at Sam's at Dirt Pot for a final gulp of Scotch whisky
And Annie and me slept up there and I made stew from lap of lamb
I let the fat settle on the surface and then skimmed it off to make it clear
so the carrots and mushrooms wouldn't be clouded much to her curly-haired
surprise and delight and then we twined our toe-boats and gondolas in
                                                          the firelight

I look upon these times with the greatest affection
These times of trout tickling and learning how to shoot a gun
Are so old now at Sparty   they just fade away on the gentlest of breezes

But these were important times   Mysterious blazing and true

Août 1997
After Apollinaire

Memories Are Made of This

      Two licorice lakes
           Catcleugh and Kielder
                 fed with dark burnwater
                       and Jackie's nightie drying on the line

Garth Hudson opens the intro to Tears of Rage in 1969
And the electric voices make your eyes pop out of their sockets
It is only the small-minded who don't understand and get ploated
In their stupid and square Fairisle sweaters and accordion beards
Because **we** all dress in the finest Italian from Marcus Price & Nickleby's

When I reached home to The Laurels I admired the blue enamel oven
And there was beautiful Jewess Vivienne in a soft woollen pink suit
But the demons of memory crawled through my body & I couldn't do it
Even though she lay in my double bed all night completely naked
Except for a pair of lilac high-heeled matching
shoes   I slept downstairs   Soviet & virginal

I was a man in a new-look baggy nightshirt starched and white
Trepanned because of a starreburst in the trenchant trenches
I stood by the window and shaved and shaved away my grievous unrest
Whistling part of Milhaud's Four Seasons which I really don't know that well
Having only heard it a thousand times It seems like opera to me

You who turn to royalty instead of the ultimate truth of Marxist democracy
And to the true modernism of ideas which Pablo understands so well
There is everything to be said that the Jesus Christ Almighty wants us to
                                                       die twice
At least the Germans only invite you once to a rat-swarming grave

Août 97
After Apollinaire

Love's Swanne Song

It is said that love comes and is the Symphonie phantastique
As if a song which has passed down the centuries
A rustling noise of lost kisses now to us the famous lovers in the Odeon
Walking from café to café at the Hôtel de Ville under the darkening sky
We always cry for love Bar and Jac even in the vingtième arrondissement
Even in the shadows of the Communist town hall of which we are proud
The man and womanhood of the two heroes involved the two swannes
The differences are erected like the Eiffel Tower between us like a jetplane
Jason and the Argonauts who cares about him with his wimp lisp
All swannes die but we do not want to die alone and unloved
After we have had the wonderful warmth of the sunne on our wings
And we have swumme in the Elvet and mated forever for life
And until I move it will not be possible for us to move any more
The panthers are moaning and weeping in the jungles of the night
The rumours of our split are deafened by the rising exotic plants
But they rise through through the thickening leaves and I quell them
And see the jetblack panthers and spotted cheetahs and quell them too
The massive artillery will be upon us again today and will astonish
us with its fantastic affection hitting people right in the face and body
We will think of Dunbar's beautiful beaches and the rolling waves where
we swam And the German shells will arrive without postcards

And in the sky we will hear the song of all of the love ever in the world

After Apollinaire
Août 1997

The Illegal 2CV

At the beginning of August in the year of 1997
I was brokenhearted and bereft by my grey-eyed strawberry blonde
I rose from my bed in Dunbar shortly before the crack of dawne
In a car driven by Kev back from the Buddhism centre

I sat in the back reading the match reports That's fine by me

We stood and watched the flocks of terns leaving England
It was briefly after 5am and I was alive
I was all of a sudden in love with someone else who talked about Jesuse
She used to serve scampi and very good French fries
And Marg
Was in the front seat with her noble nose
She looked like an Empress and of course she is

We said ta-ra to Blackfriars after one coffee

Only hours later a huge flock of terns were sweeping left to right
Their taut tight wings beating the blackening sky

The salmon were rising up the falls into the pools of Wylam
Whole centuries of opposing anger were clashing together
Even the dead were stirring in their quiet slots and I was trembling

Guard dogs barking at every single corner
I walk this earth with every battle honoured in my struggling soule
They rise within me and rise again and I see them twisting through
the mountains and fountains of the defeated town squares of my heart
Through Kielder and the hamlets of Catton where the best eggs are
And Rookhope and Stanhope and by the Banks of the Allen
They come here and rape it and then leave it to die in so-called peace
The flags are out and there is a room and a sky full of brightness

People are getting on their dawn trains and they will die at their destinations
Once more they wave their morning newspapers like bonny flags
They have come from Blyth where the disease-ridden cod stir the depths
Turned into bloaters already by the great power station tidalturns

Hiding for life in the wreckage areas where ships have gone down
Above the Iraqi desert Geordie boys fight against other airmen
It is quite dizzying to think they fight at such speed
It is much higher than the terns I saw today flying west
It was almost as if they were fleeing the Norway sunne to find the Spanish one!
I loved their sharp wings and their strange way of flocking
But there was one behind all on its own and its name was Barry
Yob fights yob yes They call it Newcastle city centre
Yet some of us are almost literate and we go from bar to bar
And poetry comes to us and believe it or nor we write it down
And hits the earthe like the very tail of an unannounced comet

I still feel You know the power of poetry which arrives like mad

We used to organise trade unions and organise the universe
We stood tall upon the globe and really felt it was ours only
We thought we were laying out the Fenwick's window
And all of the farmers of Hexham would be queuing up for the sale
They would be standing there in their boots dumb with amazement
And the dogs of Carliol Place would be running them ragged

I'll never forget the time the car broke down completely lightless
We were on the old A1 and it was utterly distressing
It was before the war of the spirit between us Before catastrophe

It was after midnight it was one it was two it was three
and then you weren't there it was four and you were not there

We went past Dragonville and Belmont and arrived in Newcastle
And saw we were going to have to go and try & slaughter Germans
We turned in Grainger Street and looked at each other lost for words
This tangerine-coloured Deux Chevaux which I was driving illegally
It had brought us up the A167 to a very different world
We are both big lads and I used to play for Northumberland Schoolboys
The bad news is that we have just been made children again
And I am in a little cot with a bullet in my poet's elegant head

Août 97
After Apollinaire

The Garden Door is Open On the World

Tonight Pearl shines beautifully and there is only one cloud as a shawl
as the rich rowan berries are Christmas red and will soon be autumn
yellow and the leaves will fall like strange rain
But Pearl and me will understand We have been there so many times
At the East Allen River the magpies bobbed and nodded sucking hen eggs
And we shot them with a .303 up here called a woman gun
Just to make sure that with the bacon from Nichol's farm we saved some
And then I took you tickling trout and we exchanged fastfingers
And the eye glances were quite astonishing one after the other
The snipe with one wing flies in a circle and then falls to the ground
I think we had better telephone its grieving mother
We are all in a terrible state birds and beasts and lousy poets
There is weeping in the branches and we are all doing it over Gran
The stupid Quayside accountants wipe the sweat with crass ties
I say raise the blind raise the dead raise the halt and lame
We walk into light through the open windows in the café
And the light is built by a series of ingenious insects
Then beauty fell upon us all A cobalt mantle indigo endless
Rescue will come eventually I hope Midnight always at hand
The time when Robert Johnson stepped on the bus
I remember your pairs of shoes under the tallboy
Especially the golden sandalettes you bought for Rachel's wedding
Pearl wandered the marigold beddes unheard by the world
She was entirely in black because she was disgraced in the Allen Valley
by the strange policemen of Jesus from the parish committee
We sat beneath the creaking trees loving our life away before love
The big rammes at Hexham are doing what they do best ramming
So the ewes have gone berserk up on the top fields aching to be tupped
And the green plovers are sweeping over the new pasture and calling
Where Sammy the poacher has brought home even more fresh rabbits
Which he unveils from the darkness of his Methodist overcoat
And being the good lad in the family I get the rabbit's kidney on Sunday
O Toronto where the blowing snow is beautiful but makes us
think it's spring with fresh buds O Newcastle in steamy summer
From the rowan to the holly high up on the Kielder banks it goes
Paris Monterey Nice Cannes Bordeaux and Saint Mark's Place

and the brilliant sunny beaches and crescents of tremendous Antigua
There is a clementine outside of the window facing west
It is the sunne It is the sunne It is the unbroken daylight whatsoever sunne

Big Mac
Août 1997
After Apollinaire

Forget About Her She Does Not Exist

for Stephen Bierley

    Morning again
And the rain falls into the trenches of the hearte
The artillery has been blown to bits
    We are blitzed and bombed sorted and invaded
But resisting everything
                    all the shards of attempted broken spirit
    Fight back against the invasions which attempt to smash Thee
When You think nowt remains
There is an inner strength which flies like a seagull or partridge
    Fast from the thickness of the heather or the edge of the Farnes
Into the wildness of the Aire
It is only September
                 yet mornings delay their coming
    And there are no summer days in England again
You can tell this by the big rivers   dry
as my mouth
I worry about the salmon and the spawning beds for this new season
Rain belts down upon the chocolate peppermint and the flowering
             lemon balm
    O Jesuse
What shall we do against the conquests and attacks
    There is only one God and he has turned his back against us
September 7am and still almost dark
What is happening to the world

Come on lads! Come on! Up out of those camp-beds!
We must quell the enemy and destroy them.
We must not mistake the Milky Way for the shells which light our night!
Dim the lamplights: don't give the snipers a target
                at which to fire.
Listen: There will be a time when once again We see the snowy owl
and the red buzzard
clawing the beautiful trees
on the Dordogne
             and high in the
olive groves

The beautiful grey volcanic rocks still belong to us
They are ours
Remember your loved ones
And if we are defeated your children will be killed
or held in capture
Or gassed if you are of the wrong racial quality
What a joke

No joke lads
We must punish and fashion all of them into deathe
No quarter

Poet Yes
But I weare a starre in my hearte
and I want you to see it
and follow me through the barbed wire
Ignoring the smoke
I wish to slaughter the enemy
just as I need to write poems
There is absolutely no difference

It is like love
The desire for victory will never die

Under death and fortitude
And the terrible clouds of invasion which never winne
Against all of this beautiful freedom already in the world

Septre 97
Inspired by Apollinaire

At the Hoppings
for Anthony and Fiona

    after Apollinaire

Steel tricks bust our skulls
They're elegant bright & smash us in
    Make them Go on then German engineer

The fight between grace and bravery

Black Swiss ski-pants
Rising livewire over the barbed wire
    Like a white silk Northumberland Street Fenwick bra that you
  unhook
There isn't a moment like it
I LOVE IT   THE WHITENESS OF cloudes
        Write it on my headstone

Poets stalking Kielder
    Through larches and other abstract trees
I've known you so long since Buxton   Indifference   Is a stranger
        His plucky gunne almost stops me dead
Even the withering roses give hope to my hearte
Then I go to hospital and don't know my heade

Because I dream of the roses of other places
Where they bloom unblemished by headwounds
O my love   O my love   O my great verity Thee also a rose
Dollywobbles   Your hips spread out wide

I breathe alcoholism into the air
Then the starres and argent sky swoon through my filters
And the shells hit our skulls
This beautiful trenchwater   This gorgeous meadow
Stricken by artillery

      I rise up in polished black boots
      Which I polished myself because we received supplies

The roses are red and we die too

But the roses will eventually winne

Septre 97
Just before the Hellhound Train Never Ending Tour
From Guillaume's Fête

I Don't Walk the Line All of the Time

You don't know what
You don't know what
You don'tknow fuckall
You don't know the fall
                                    back from the brink
The journey from the ball
                                        to the endless drinke

Get a load of it
,my children
                                                      I'm flat out loaded

If the logs fall from the fire
I'll burn to death
Sacrifice a final breath

Autumn now and the leaves are falling like poems
                                  onto the pages of the pavements
War is everywhere and the dead are dead or dying
And the conspiracies
Never cease
                           They lie on crispest sheets white and blue
Where is my brother tonight

I long for him to be well and better
and care not for myself
I give up my own care
I collapse it into the earthe
I balloon it to the sky
That he should leave the trenches of his inner-war
I don't care
Yes I do
Because I love a woman very special
She wears a mustard shirt
I touched it even
Cherise denims and brown sandals
Those little toes pointing out

Peachy Tremendous Absolutely   Splendid

A bonus like Rain

Septre 97 After Guillaume

All of Your Sinnes Will Be Known Always and Never Forgiven

The seamist has risen from the Arctic roses and from the lemon balm
    and is now replaced by the bright Northumberland sunshine of August
Long live France I say or you'll end up in a bed dead and then a coffin
    And who wants to be a stiffo in the Père Lachaise in the 20th
next to Edith Piaf Oscar Wilde and that strange bloated man bad poet
                                                            Jim Morrison
    But all of your sinnes are known by Jesus and unless you renounce them
you will never be in a position to stalk the earth and tell a poet's truth
    I sleep in my wee bed of a soldier facing death from rifle and Zeppelin
I do not want to lie next to the bullet holes which slaughtered the
                                                            Communards
    I'd prefer to die in the arms of my beloved heroine Lou who also
                                                            speaks poetry
Yet trepanned I am grateful to Doctor Brennan who brought me back to
                                                        life I will be eternally
dedicated to Sister Susan with her blue uniform & white strategic gloves
    Now that I have gone awry crooked askew lopsided off-centre
                                                              unsatisfactory
And hammer the hardmetal of the streets without completing my various
                                                              responsibilities
Except spitting in the gutter at the former headmaster who tried to
                                                                   pederast me
    There are times when you don't complete
And later it is a long time of regret   Pablo speaking of me on his death-bed

to be finished
due to complete exhaustion
Au 97
after the main man

Petition to the Jesus Christ Almighty

                Just a bairn
        And I stalked the back lanes of Walker
           opposite the Neptune Naval Yard
             with my little camera
         and blue overalls with straps
               destined for fame
Even then I spoke to the Virgin Mary as a friend
and said my prayers at night before blessed sleep
        and the latest round of shelling
          And asked Jesus to love me forever
      I knew I would love Thee till I die a swanne
        And yet the endtime has appeared like a bomb
but I do not believe in the cerulean blue of Italian heaven
              or the infinite crimson of German shellhole hell
I cast my beliefs aside I cast aside all doctrines and philosophies
 I will never subscribe to anything ever again except charcoaled flags
      The seaman who was picked up in the choppy waters
             off the Black Middens
starved freezing and hungry but near the headquarters of the NUS
 because he always wore a cross and silently said his prayers
        He looked like me he looked like me he was me

after Apollinaire
Août 97

Annie

At the shores of Whitley Bay
Between the Black Middens and Blyth
My huge garden overgrown and cascading with Victorian tea roses
My gorgeous little house
a tremendous overblown rose in itself
O darling I miss your letters from Hollywood

And our pony-tailed dances in the Methodist hall

Often you stalked elegant and alone
among the roses of the church garden
And I passed gazing after you
longing and longing for love of you
longing and longing for your dancing feet
We looked at each other Annie as if there was no tomorrow

O Annie don't join the Methodists
for God's sake
Look at the rosetrees and leave on your buttons
and don't become a Mennonite
There is only one law no clothes for lovers   And shells and war
If you are going to take off your buttons
join me in some strange club
One's just dropped off my new Nickleby's reefer jacket
does that mean we worship the same Christ?

There is nothing grimmer than this grim darkest of nights
except perhaps Mons
There will be nothing darker than endless and relentless as death itself
The German tracers will never stop until all my comrades do

after Apollinaire

Entrance to Heaven

The door of the Hotel Armstrong grins like an insomniac maniac
In the decent and quiet avenue of the Communist 20th arrondissement
Where we are falling completely in and out of love again darling
Mam what does this mean for me other than a trip towards death
Wylam rail bridge so far away now and the salmon spawning beds
just upstream from the Rocket Angling Club's private fishing banks
She became an icy angel an advocate of winged sensibility
I still listen to her lips on the telephone singing her distant song
Just for love of it and then it and my heart dies and dies
I am abashed cheapened devalued and completely debased
I am an arrow-ridden zero on the last pub dartboard in Alston
I am in the Angel Inn and not one cherub will speak to me
The German artillery at least want to communicate wounding death
Listen Bar I taught you to read and write opposite the Neptune Yard
At the age of three and four the rest of the world is poetry so live & work

After Apollinaire
Août 1997

The Dollbird/Redblonde

after Apollinaire

I stand in front of you all despite it all I'm still sensible, straight-tongued
I understand everything about life and death because I've been
and am still on the fringes of both
Two wives and a million women one after the other
I convinced others notably newspaper employers and union colleagues
to follow my way of thinking and then it seems I suddenly failed
I know French, some Italian, no German, who would want to
except to appeal to them to stop shooting their monumental artillery
I have been in a million places: Paris, the Cevennes,
Cannes, Gloucester, Massachusetts, St Mark's Place with the
late Allen Ginsberg but never Denver Colarado
I was wounded in the head in the heart in the souls of the mind
and went on the drip because of the alcoholism which hangs my brain
I lost everyone Allen Ed Mark they all went the complete distance
The people I unkindly wanted to go wouldn't leave this earth
I did not have a gunne it was hopeless I wanted them to go NOW
I will have to detach myself from this warre between thee and me
I will have to disattract myself from your 4 lipstick prints on the walle
There is a great notice in the Sky: this is the order this is the new idea
I had this terrible moment of shame I couldn't remember his name
then it returned like a flurry of gunfire   I was abashed in forgetfulness
You think you speak in God's words I don't think so
When you've been on the Heminevrin drip you really do know better
the entyre universe
you wait all night long for people to stop playing Hank Williams in your
                                                                      brainbox

Swan Hunter asbestosis victims
men from the shut collieries
Unknown bonfires of the heart
Rainbows never seen
Unrenounced dreams of Clare

Kindness will be investigated and hopefully a newly-peaceful country
We will retrieve time
we will not

We're on the borders night and day shooting at enemies we do not know
it is the end of time and the time of the future
at the same time
Pity us
Pity us
our mistakes are as big as our terrible sinnes

The relentless upheavals of summer come upon us with Pearl in the
meadows of Sparty
some say it is a time of violence with the bursts of the flowers
my childhood lies in tatters beneath the apple trees

O my darling sunshine wake before me let me sleep
my springtime as in Milhaud is corrupt completely
I thought reason had a chance but now I know better

I'm waiting sweetheart I think your name is Kelly
I'm hanging about to follow the sweetest form there is
And you Kelly will walk through the streets of Newcastle
with everything hanging off you like antlers

And every night I will be magnetised to your bedroom
The dollbird with the square high-heels and the ruby locks
Her hair is argent it is so brisky frisky and buoyant
A torchlight a lighthouse going on into eternity

Victorian tea-roses from the garden which haunt
the world with their hearth and heartlike flames

They never fade in a paradisal slow parade of death
They have always an eternal sweetness of nature's breath

Go on take the piss all of you take the mick
I know everything and if I told you you'd go the distance
     So many items of a various nature you would not want

Mercy ache tenderness
Unbelievable sanity
lay them in the courtyard at my door

And pity me forever for what I know
                about everyone and the complete universe

Juillet 97
after Apollinaire

Listen It's Plutting
for Caroline Calvert

Then	sol	of	con	O
l	diers	Flan	fuse	My
ist	houn	ders	the	Sparty
en	ded	o	en	rain
to	lo	ur	emy	so
the	st	a	hor	ten
mus	in	go	izon	der
ick	the	ny	wi	my
of	lim	under	th	Dirt
the	bs	the	gunn	Pot
fall	of	rain	es	pluts
ing	a mill	pl	th	you
rain	ion	ea	ough	ta
so	art		the	sty
lo	illery	se	al	as
der	hor	rain	most	m
so	ses	stop	in	y
swee	be	eve	visible	lo
t	neath	n	lace	ve
	the	so	mist	
	cres	swee	is	
	cent	t	so	
	moo		swee	
	n		t t	
			oo	

Horse intestines are spilled on the path
    So long   gun-trenches
We WILL recover them
we will retrieve the Front
With gun-cunning
As we gaze sadly into the hell shell-holes
Filled with the blood and guts
Of horses and comrades

The Germans have ended the ceasefire
   Don't you see We won't come back again
         I am the poet of the trench
And dead in the helmethead I will not come back

    To the
    Pe
    ris
    co
    pe

  To check the enemy trenches
            We don't want France to die

  The Club a Gogo which smashes
  the silence of night
  with Muddy Waters and Jimmy Reed
  Bright Lights Big City

   Like the German shells

A wild beck in the sky

Don't stuff the beaks of the birds with child cotton
      Don't attract your heart with extra pain
   And to the kisser of the flagge
And the walker of miles from Elba
Say
      Helllo
He brought France into the modern age
I am France and France is Me!

But as the shelles deluge and spate
Everything is demented now
       Here   where we lads are

Septre 97/Mars 98
After Apollinaire

Letter from Guillaume Apollinaire to Barry MacSweeney

My dear fellow poet
Life is so difficult you can go from bad to verse
Tonight the German tracers filled the sky like starres
Bar it is a complete tragedy that you are there and I am here
and I am in a rainsodden trench and that you are not
I don't enjoy it believe me I prefer my stylish Paris shoes
striding up to Montmartre to have a chat with Pablo my best mate
O goodness Bar the bombardments have begun again it's pouring down
                                                  on the trenches
You're dead lucky only the North Sea mist is seeping in on you
Out here beyond Brittany before ferries were invented
we are under the Bosch cosh
fantastically thickened to the very earth of the universe
And once more the tracers fill my eyes like the skies
and like the orange lights beneath the tyres as you walk along Rookwood Road
My fellow poet
don't despair at the non-appearance of your book
you know that it will appear one day
We may both be dead
but the lights in the sky
and the brilliant shadows under the wheels
of these tremendous modern cars

In the trenches

Secret Poem Number Nine

for SJL

I questioned—on the first time we made love—whether you
      trimmed your quim hair and you said no—
And I have always thought you a complete idol ever since
      You are like a female Elvis Aaron to me under a Graceland sky
I'm a crackerjack wacky Jacky myself chopping down women
      O my red 4 kissprints on the wall of my study
What am I carp in your pond a trout in your running becks and streams?
      You my gong my siren my bells of St Mary The Kindred
I have walked the snowladen peaks all of my life looking for thee
      You are the snow-filled hills and fells and the law of Alston
I seek your wonderful mouth with my gorgeous bow and arrow
      And you will be my darling collector of silk & steel flesh
I will use my crampons to haul myself into your sun-brightened hairlocks
      You are the various swivelling spit vessels on the canals of my kisses
And the lily we brushed against each other's intimate most personal parts
      In the most erotic moment of our now broken lives
O my apple and pear trees are filling with good fruit
      And the sweet suckling of your breasts
under your bra gone for good from one broken blue guitar string to another
      There is a light in the sky almost a torch of sheer flame
And it is a zero pronouncement it is a useless arrangement we don't even have
      A retirement from life   a doomed cult   Lipstick traces now only no
                                                Yes sir none Sir!
The kind of Tarantino quarantino beloved by medics
      Blood guts brains on the ground no love ever again Only war

Juillet 97/Mars 98
after Apollinaire

1997

My eternal love—the one who tells me our souls
are knit
wears a fantastic lilack silk suit from New Bond Street
bought especially for a trip to a poetry reading in Devon
And she wears those gold sandalettes bought for Rachel's wedding

Her eyes prom flirt flutter and waltz like cherubs
She laughed and giggled in the café
La Tourelle   plats du jour
Our hearts and toes were I thought forever twined
The complete colours of Paris flew into our hearts
It was the revolution all over again
The guillotines and the knitting were in our very minds
The wonderfully useful cobblestones

As we stayed in the vingtième arrondissement
the only Communist one in Paris
Stephen says
What a pure choice

Her lilac suit with its fresh collar
Hair done at Fenwick's
Arms swathed in brilliant sunlight and Verlaine rain

We never heard midnight we were in the Hôtel de Ville

She trailed the boulevards in those golden shoes
And I fell in love with her again and again
and again
Up the Tower
into the atmosphere of the clouds

She is foxy, peachy, magnificent gorgeous beyond belief
I dared to love her and she broke me heart

There have been some horrendous encounters in tremendous cities
With the throngs of new children
Iron and steel in the veins
but at least complete flamebrains
I loved 1968 the Citroën workers showing me car parts
In the shelves ready to throw at gendarmes
Everything is useless like beauty and luxuriants

She is so gorgeous
She terrifies me

*

Juillet 97
After Apollinaire

Rue Christine Lundi

Nation, The Square of the Overturned Throne
Where we put the guillotine
It's far more than we did in England
Except once which was not enough
The Hotel Armstrong in Communist 20th arrondissement where you can buy
harissa opposite the street market filled with beautiful fresh vegetables
And it was like a honeymoon even though we are not married
Keep the stile open while Pearl climbs through
and flitflights her way to the borage groves

We have electricity at last in the Loaning Head
It's been connected
And now you can read we can read together at night
The owner of the beautiful café is gasping for breath
I went to Tunis with a woman I thought beautiful until I met Thee

and I recognised personal wonderfulness for the first time
I bought red hot peppers next to the Rue Bourguiba
and kept them for years
but when I met Thee
you were hotter than Africa
It might be a fascist place but it has a lot of style

In the Hotel Armstrong the Germans are holding up the queues
And the coffee is lukewarm and sour
But the rain of Paris is sweet and you are writing your best poems

We're leaving at 9.15
And I'm most protective of my absolute heart
Which I wish to save for you

There's a mirror in the bathroom of the Hotel Armstrong
Which reminds me of Tyneside and Vickers
There's a mixed-up confusion between us
You taunting beautifully-breasted scallywag woman

There is a wild spirit in you I try to catch like a kite
My new coat protects me from the chill rain
And the black and white cat is stalking the floor

The buns and blueberry cheese were tremendous
And in Alston the taps are running waiting for us
But I don't understand <u>black as her nails</u>

The ground is a circus filled with animals
The redhead in the bookshop was abducted and sold to the world

Listen Jac this is serious   My love for you is laid down in silver and gold

The train the Tunnel I wrote about for years

We travelled through it and dozed as if it did not exist

The mind in my brain—imagine!—said Can we prod the little maid
towards you No I don't want her I want the best woman poet in England
Her name is Jackie Litherland I stand by it I am its protector

I have bought a painting by Rachel Levitas—the daughter of the best
woman poet alive in England   and am as proud as Punch
The Temptation of St Anthony and I am in it borne aloft by Demons

Stockhausen says   Ignore the known world
I agree
You are the greatest living woman poet in England
so acknowledge yourself
and stand tall in the world
as you should
your absolutely rightful place

Juillet 97
inspired by Apollniare

Treasure

For SJ Litherland

Always long time live my undying love
A princess of golden hair ashblonde
In which nation? I don't know darling.
Long time past lives my love long time
Cost of exotic fruit forever your enemy
It will alter the treasure of your beauty
If we let it, long time my gorgeous lover
My princess of the bullion bargol

There is a treasure buried under the earth
The mere cost of the iris petals we rubbed
Tries to temper our beauty quite lately
Through Irish cloakclasps discovered in peat
Beauty's eye plutting alone in the sad rain
She cries she weeps she oars without solace
In a Spanish king's ransom buried under sand
And it is the time of the rubbing of the iris petals

Of your downy moss I am the dawning fire
Murmured and murmuring to the bed queen
Merle song, chant of the whisperer, sunriselark
Your foam beaches against the rough grain of my chin
Hair twined and turned in electric blue forget-me-nots
Such poverty! Yet you're a wonder among all women
I am the ticket collector of your hanky-wiped tides
Green-breasted plovers upon your royal tongue

This is by a young man—24—and devoted to you
Who will be handkerchiefing your drying-up eyes
How did the fairy of morning reply to the ring-ousel?
Beside the brave harpist who is nailed to your heart
Who your daughter says She thinks the world of you
Beside us you despise the Auroroa Borealis of gold
By the eternal mod in pressed pants who adores you
And who dedicates his life to stop you crying anymore

Ten years of celibacy I waited princess JacLou
Then one day she telephoned and we laughed & laughed
Horsewoman through the empty collieries whip-stirruped
—ten years waiting for the Leveller pizza gossip talker—
Plucky, advancing of the heart, rich without venal cash
Who plundered the stark booty of my heart took it for hers
Ten years in monkish dereliction before Palace Green
Then it was her day her favour on my jousting lance

The poor darling three years in the Halls of Hell
Lovecask wrapped in a purse of dried leather;
The poor darling even though Midlands sensible
So lovable but not loved decently & quite invisible.
One-night sad plunderers boasting invincibilities
Tried to take the purse and boast it their stupid own
The woman in the Halls of Hell would not have it
And the loveflagon remained her own integrity & charm

She wept because of the bondaged body she slept in
But you know it was not necessary to cry day or night
The perils of North Sea winds dislodged the slates
—She would moan and weep in a state of physical indenture—
One man thought he could enter the house causing carnage
But he was nothing but a one-night stand murderer
Once again she plied her eye to tears of loneliness
But that man was not worth it and she stood with all her will

Her real love from the Halls of Hell, Mr Celibacy
declared:—I'm the man you want! And I want you too.
But I have been lately mad. I am a shootable mad bullock,
Jeus complex perhaps, celibate as the Great Almighty,
Nothing I like better than a half bottle of wine.—
Now LouJac pops her head round the kitchen door
Finding the spineless stupid saviour—so-called—poet
muttering: I really have all the treasure I need now

That's the tribetale. Dear friend. Of the Queen of the Halls
of Hell. My name? Finnba Failure. I'm not saying the real one.
And your true biography my moon-kissed, iris-stroked friend?
I have told the recent vita, the Treasure of the Sierra Madre,
All my enemies want my oil-well derricks, the Boche want my head.
None of you can have any of it. The whole treasure is for my
petlamb, dewdrops in her hair from the laurel leaves. Trim
haired crown of laurel leaves upon her laureate's brow.

April 25 1999
From Apollinaire's
Le Trésor

Lou's the name on my lips

Wolves of every kind in the night
I know them inhuman beyond belief
The demon devil steals my heart
And he dumps it at his doorway
It's just a bairn's toy in his hands

Older wolves were more faithful to me
As are the smaller bowsie-wowsies
And the amorous soldiers in love with the babes
The women an elegant wonderful memory
In the same way as the wolves are sweet

But today times really are worst of all
The nightmare wolves are now tigers
And the infantry and the fascist Empires
The Caesars have turned into Vampires
Harshly cruel as our shell-rising Venus

Bye bye Rouveyre I'm leaving now
Climbing astride my giant horse
I am going soon heading for war
Without pure mercy & hawk-eyed severity
Just like the trench warriors of Epinal

Selling it off as a popular image
That Georgin was hyping in the the forest
Where are they those beautiful soldiers
Soldiers lost dog-tags Where are the wars
Where are the blitzkriegs of yesterday

Oct 12 98
p79 Calligrames
C'est Lou qu'on la nommait

Letters to Dewey

(1999)

Roses and Petroleum

He walked down the street with the keen step of a man wanting to reach his next drink.

The sky in the west, over the hills, was a wondrous rose, though not chilled, because the earth here was warming up after the rigours of Christmas.

Three things on his mind: the dislocation of his kid brother's marriage to a sister-in-law he loved deeply, the complete fracture of his life-long love—and the distressing fascination with reaching the store on the corner of the road before the offy closed at ten.

Here is a man with a thousand grievances—at least—a man with a twisted gravestone face. He knows there are only crumbs left in his soul, whatever that is, and his only sheer purpose is to count the cash again and make sure there's enough to make sure the young cuckoos in his slightly inert system don't start beaking for profound feeding by 11 p.m.

The precise moment the man had said on the box. All moments are precise he thought otherwise they would not be moments, i.e., less than seconds, less than minutes, far less than hours, shorter than a day, a weekend, a long weekend, in Blackpool perhaps, Burnley, Bradford, or Barnet High Street, not to mention Folkestone sea front, and certainly shorter than a year, not to mention a millennium.

Shakespeare was probably packing into a rocket salad before we even heard about it in between him writing Romeo and Juliet with his pasta and fruit.

Winter Hill Chardonnay. Nice as ninepence. Coverage, overage, over age, covert cages, rages over the top, manage, cove herald of free enterprise, enter if you want a prize, prise it open if you will or must, nice one, can you spell, reject?

Page two follows next but it's all in the same size and he'd just received a telephone call from the United States of America.

Out in Brooklyn, the beat goes on. Quay Street. Dewey Rodefer picks up a telephone for the first time in the land of the free. And makes funny very loud noises drowning out the background of traffic, police cars, the aftermath of murder, and hungry dogs bothering the stragglers in between the half-eaten rejected burgers.

Hi Dewey.

2

Dewey dear there are many hard and indeed difficult and different things you hear in this world. One is musick but the rest are words and of course the depraved news which is rubbish money by people who claim to be born-again Christians. They aren't and even if they are they are worse than the Serbs in the feasts of the forests of the frozen nights.

Dear Dewey I am honoured and overwhelmed with tears because in the Western universe of great conversation technology as the European frontiers began its new muscle-spending onslaughts that you lifted up that great thing—the Yankee telephone—for the first time and mimicked to me with a voice which told me many things. I was talking to your father when your sweet young voice intervened.

Dewey, it was the first time you had responded to a telephone except in pure sound. You're not my son, but I am honoured.

3

The rhythm circus had not yet been put into place and position. It was slightly out of place.
It was a grand idea and felt really good in prospect.

Spectacles off, there was nothing more to say.

4

There are many brilliant and divine things: strange alliterations corrected, beast fervour controlled, flowers in the dark of night, Mediaeval music which spares the mind the barebones of our current existence in the skeletons of depravity.
But listen Dewey.

5

Enjoy, and enforce your enjoyment in an English manner, cardboard, coriander, and conduits, and when a daffodil laughs in your face when you first see one don't be scared—it's telling you it isn't a sunflower, although it will seem tall to you.

There are taller things. Forests and people. But already you are as high as forests all the way to California and as high as chateaux in the grandness of Francedom. And the people, of which you are now one.

They're unbelievable.
And so are you.

6

The only mystery in an Elastic band on the street stirred by early summer wind is that somebody held it before letting it fall. How gorgeous and beautiful! Not just the band—made in a strange country you will get to know and it may be your own—but the person, man or woman, that they may now be unwrapping a packet, once-wrapped, which contains a gift.
It may contain their whole life.

7

Believe in trout and the fishing of them and the yellow of forsythia when eventually it becomes impossible to gaze at.

So travel and look at wheat.

Always believe in airplanes. Ride them like motorbikes. Trains are beautiful but faster is better. And television is eternal, just like books and people and kindness.

8

There are many informers, traitors and some will be Presidents and friends.
Don't forgive them, but deliver justice like a man.

9

Always keep a spare lightbulb handy.

10

The American Marines are beautiful whereas English poetry walks a strange and weird road.

Listen to recordings of B-52s—you'll get them from the Capitol on the Mound.

Technology is fantastic, grand, and enduring. Not a god.
Or be a SEAL and shave your head down to the bone.

11

There are many lies. People wear bears and don't shave—and that includes the women—and they write and paint and play musick in a way you will find either acceptable or not or with which you will let pass by or be bored beyond belief.
Rumours, too, like snakes, invade this world, and whirl across the human-made dust. They, when the wind blows from the incorrect direction, morally that is, will set to blind, and that is then to perchance against it and them and not be fallen or be slighted or have a mote within your eyes.

Reject fumery and tomfoolery. Don't wear your cap back to front.
Expect everything.
And when it comes, send it back with the most terrible vengeance upon your hand.

12

Expect nothing.
It will arrive at whichever door you have.
There are many odd circumstances, and they are to be respected, like tinned grapefruit, or pineapple, for example, and they will not go away.
Be stern.

13

Famous days will approach and maintain rapprochements within themselves. They are often difficult to approach. Look at raptors and listen to the howling of hounds.

And always understand French because it is the key between the Tour Eiffel and Jackson Pollock and Frank O'Hara and the motor industry of Chicago. And then stand upright under each brilliant skyscraper—made by men and women of the country of your birth—and realise

I LIED AND I SAID I DID WITH A SMILE ON MY FACE

14

Broken fingernails—right hand, middle finger—are only part of the human atlas.

So have many vitamins and at all costs avoid Indonesian leaders putting their own hands together in what turns out to be a signal of mock prayer while their police outside are beating the people to a gas-peppered pulp.

Please avoid the gas yourself.

Now listen Dewey.

And this is imperative.

Hassle all strangely offhand officials until they come around to your way of thinking, be polite but firm, and the world might alter slightly back towards humanity.

Our way.

There are also strange investments to be made, often after midnight, which many times is the brightest time, and the sunne will soon rise upon whatever parterres you have near you and your beautiful parents.

There are also strange winds, singular instruments, disgusting adornments, but you will see the truth of these at last and will be free, rinsed of sinne.

15

You'll have great snow in Brooklyn and Paris and its interpretations in England where it can be quite soft in the meadows of southern England where even Shelley walked. I saw his hair once.

Delight in his verse.
Ignore the warmasters.
When the snow falls here, and then the sun fills the sky, it feels like a truly wonderful world. Then it will be time for a proper Christmas.

16

There will be grief make no mistake but a hands-on grip of life will be the one pure and simple request for a future in control. That's not soft. Struggle in the ditches and walkways, sure, but survive forever.

17

Hogmanay. Gillian. Log fires burning. Pearl by the hearth.
She will have her baby and she will be well after.

18

Always be innocent and suspicious. Treat the given as it is. The squares on television are mere squares.
When the sun shines upon your upturned face, laugh as you walk to school. Listen to banjos.

19

Listen Dewey, I am a common man. I am common as muck. I am the original muck-spreader after farmers Noble and Nicholl who built their ginormous leeks up here in the high grounds and we all sat around and read Zane Grey when the fires died and we were dead asleep until the lentils and the beasts the next dawn.
Being a common man is most special.
What you have to do is turn it.

20

You nerd, you seedstalk, you droneatic. Wake up! It's Sunday!

And THAT goes back in the fridge.

21

    Exasperation is a word that strays, Dewey, between the beautiful bluebells. Then the flowers die.
    But of all language lives on and on and on.
    However don't ever despair. It will return.
    The sun rises on the United States every morning.
    Isn't it gorgeous, there, through the haze?

22

    When stretching out in the aromatic automatic water feel free to do what you like. I will envy you from up here in the treeline.
    But there is no sense in envy.
    It craves and graves and eats the soul.
    This is not for you, thee, bright telephone lad.
    You are different.
    Look at that button in the rushing Quay Street rain.
    It's as bright as you are.

23

    Learn word-irons, ring words, and be brass bold. Always adore the sky.

24

    There is no co-operation and red cars are vile. So far away and so many handkerchiefs.
    Learn the essential use of wardrobes, corridors, doors, windows, useless ornaments, condiments, pepper salt and water.

25

    The starres were out tonight despite the winds from the north west and east and Gillian spoke on the telephone.

26

Dear Dewey enjoy the subways. But also come to the Scots Lowlands. And Northumbria which is grand.

27

There was a woman I met and she won't be my bride tomorrow. She will not be my bride ever and nor will she give me a baby: too old.
The starres shone all night but she was too asleep.
She kept going to the toilet.
And still the great winds descend from the lawsz and meanz.

28

I have never met you but I love Brooklyn and New York and Manhattan.
Gillian will love it too.
Don't use anything stronger than a 4lb breaking strain, probably with a dun fly [enclosed]. Home-made.
And only in spring.

29

How was the fishing today? And how was school?
Gillian said, through beautifully pursed lips, I'll
disguise it as I did.

30

So she did it and it was fine and adorable. We all suffer from streams of expenditure that are the blood of the nation. Ah, it doesn't matter. There are necessary waves of knowing with which we have to come to tennis. And we do.
Dewey, when she pursed her lips, I fell to bits, right beside the telephone.
Dewey, she clicked her heels and I died nine times. There was electric fire in the soul. Distress mixed with enormous love and tenderness and

faith. And of course, there was rain. Otherwise it would not be Paris or Queens or the Bronx or Brooklyn or the whole rest of New York.

Nails follow.

31

When the nails come, ignore their lancinating effects upon the flesh. It's a mindless attack and control of capitalism at its highest and some say its worst. Affect your own critique and build your thoughts on standards set by Frank.

Listen Dewey, there are quiet places, too. Beyond Quay Street.
Find them.
The world is a mix, various, fantastic, wild, natural, calm, disgusting, milk, beast musick, famous nothings, teachers of nowhere, and always gorgeously beautiful and elegant.
There is so much to seek and find.

32

Remember your cartilages.
It's half-past one and it might as well be 18-minutes past four.
There are times in enchantment.
They.

33

Don't ever take a cabbage to a vet.

34

Or feed it to the goose.
Many strange sorrows lie ahead of us, driven by the sand.
What's gone before us is always total life.
There are no more easy days.
Our sentences have been shortened, unfortunately.

35

It's raining in New York.
The gem-knot tie which will abominate you as much as me from the former Yugoslavian security chief will always make us pleased on Boxing Day.
It too is lying in the dark.

36

I saw the water towers and the sun was rising over the buildings. Astonishing.

37

Collapse. Failure. Ignoring the lure of capitalist success. Rising again, following the bee to the flower.
It's a law and a lore.
And where the bee sleeps, there sleep you.
The naval yards are all empty now.
I saw them.

38

Here we are in the don't-give-a-toss department supplying some attempt to understand the word probably.

39

I'm stupid enough to try and get through. But then again I'm intelligent enough to do so.

Along with the fierce fire I have gone with the night and my beard.

40

Knuckle. Bright features. Snow in the snow. Peace at first. And last.
Kisses.
Interruption.

41

    She should not have had our daughter
aborted. It was her decision only.
Her name was Bonny.

42

    The pressure, the pressure, and the sweet green grass of beautiful Miltonic England.

43

    All lips tell lies. But don't lie to yourself. And even if you do, forever resist the will not to love.

44

    See St Bride 1913
              by John Duncan
1866–1945
              tempera on canvas
122.3 by 144.5 cms

There is a seal on the left
and two angels holding a woman with long ashblonde hair.
They are flying as angels do
and the woman is praying.

45

    There are many deceits, rumours and false notions.
    Yet to rise against them is not by chance the greatest of things we can do.
    Always do it, my dear friend's son.

    And never refuse your milk or school sandwiches.

46

Dewey, once I had stones in my left-hand shoe.
I could have tuned to the Jesus Christ Almighty
but I took off my shoe with both hands and removed them myself.
Angels touched me on my shoulders instead.
I walked tall ever since, notably in Northumberland and Manhattan.

47

Now the lady in my moon has gone. That Pearl, that perle. Let them all talk about her, she's still my Pearl.
For good.

48

There are many pearls, and Pearls, and they lie by stiles and daffodils and hide within the flowers.
Parts depart, the skies break open and the sun looks down upon us with a brazen grin as if a golden clock.
As if a dandelion way above the cover of the cumulus.
In jet planes I delight at it once again as we rise into the sky. Pretty Pearl cannot be here today, her passport has been cleansed.
She likes the busy runways if we fly inland.
We have fallen in love again though it is a thing of the past. My dearest dearest Pearl my darling shrugger, us potato diggers with our hands must stick together in the dirt.
Hold me, dear.

49

Dearest squeak voice, young Buddy Holly, James Brown, smack my chops, clop my clappers, clop, my clappers, ham my milk, yarn my silk, frisk my tune and cure my burn.

50

Lay your heart upon the earthe.

for Dewey Rodefer 1999

False Lapwing

O raptor inside the deciduous tree leaves
Berry-beaking birds in the season of holly
    and gifts to family and friends and of charades
    If only my children would run to me from
the darkness and my unborn daughter
I droop my poor weakened brains and weep
    for loss of them into the endless nights
    I'm waiting for them to turn up forever
So I can tuck them in and read made-up tales
And stories of high hills and becks and streams
    Here is a set of six nature knowledge books
    Beautiful and green-backed But who But who
shall I give them to now my unseen ghosts
I drag my wings as the clock speeds up and the moon rises
    If only it would shine into your face
    An illuminated opal in the shawl of cot-time
A father should always respect his little bairns
And read to them until they fall into sleep & safety
    I don't now own a domestic corridor
    reduced terribly in all circumstances
And I will never go to Boots again to buy
a dummy for baby talcum to ease the little rashes
    My soul reduced and modified to a strange
    foreign condition without bounty of dadhood
O my lost love what did we do wrong as the buntings
flashed in the Kielder pathways and pecked the earth
    It seemed every symphony and sonata we could
    think of was jam-packed into our oceanic hearts.
Then against the very jagged reefs the waves swept
And the whitecaps and white horses turned joyless & jet
    Yet the children not yet seen turned their wild
    attention from the Christmas fairy lights
Flinging their slender tender arms and mitts
around us before the rush to unwind seasonal ribbons
    Yanking from the open hearth the hot scones
    While every bell in the universe gonged a carol

At midnight snow swept our ankles like a naked duvet
And Wenceslas was brought to annual life again
   The Aga dimmed in the kitchen The partridge
     not quite done But the apple charlotte perfection
And the drowsy little ones fresh from polished pews
Dozed by the blaze ready for a final tucking-in
   Laying them down we were used to ducking the mobiles
     as they squeaked echoing the bells in the Saxon belfry
And the nightlight by the semi-open pink-painted door
   reminded us we said on the stairs of the recent bonfire

Pearl Standing Alone in Sparty Moonlight

You zebra grazing in a field of horses   brilliant flaring eyes
which flash. The bed's a nowt now and the shutters open
but no more coal-dust or lead. Let us walk to the big wheel...
It's Saturday Pearl darling. It's the Bigg Market experience
It's the white cotton clothes. It's less clothes off the colder it gets.
It's the Club A'Gogo in Percy Street in Newcastle
And stand three feet from Muddy Waters and Burdon
singing She's 14 Years Old [Chess]. Just look at Consett
where the enemies of the people were where we stood on the law,
My Betty Grable My lone frozen font The way with your mouth
An exit sign
        I flash my poet's wings and you look at me outstandingly
        and starring   and staring   completely

        Soundless in the night   Tongue still as a furnace
                switch

Notes on Texts

The following information provides, where known, the place of earliest printing and notable subsequent publication. The text in this volume usually follows the first book printing: exceptions are recorded below.

The notes on the poems are intended to illuminate people and places. They are by no means exhaustive, and rarely touch on the many literary allusions, half-quotations, or puns that MacSweeney revelled in. As Basil Bunting once put it, they may perhaps allay some small irritations.

From: *The Boy From the Green Cabaret Tells of His Mother* (**London: Hutchinson, 1968; New York: McKay, 1969**).
The title sequence, comprising the poems from 'The Track, Fervour' to 'Pastoral', was circulated in mimeograph form to the mailing-list of *The English Intelligencer* in September 1967. The dates of composition supplied in the mimeo *Cabaret* are noted below. The text follows the printing in the Hutchinson edition, which is near-identical.

'autobiography of Barry MacSweeney'
Rimbaud: Arthur Rimbaud (1854–91), French poet and crucial early influence on MacSweeney.
Baudelaire: Charles Baudelaire (1821–67), French poet and writer. MacSweeney's translation of 'Le Vin du Solitaire' was published in *Workshop*, No. 12 (1971).
Laforgue: Jules Laforgue (1860–87), French/Uruguayan poet. MacSweeney translated several of his poems between 1967–73.
Basil Bunting (1900–85): poet, author of *Briggflatts* (1966), worked in the same office as MacSweeney at the *Newcastle Evening Chronicle* 1965–66. Became President of the Poetry Society in 1971; MacSweeney was Chair of the General Council, 1976–77.
Tom Pickard (1948–): poet, filmmaker, founder (with Connie Pickard) of the Morden Tower reading series which MacSweeney attended.
Jon Silkin (1930–97): poet, founder and editor of the long-running *Stand* magazine. In 1966 MacSweeney prepared an index to *Stand*, dating back to the first issue, from 1952.
Cros: Charles Cros (1842–88), French poet and theorist of photography and sound.
Corbiere: Tristan Corbière (1845–75), French poet.

'To Lynn at Work Whose Surname I Don't Know'. *Stand*, Vol. 8, No. 2 (1966).
High Level Bridge: One of the seven bridges over the river Tyne, connecting Newcastle and Gateshead. The 'staithes' are landing-stages for river traffic at the foot of the bridge. The High Level Bridge is the closest to the *Evening Chronicle* offices on Groat St, where MacSweeney worked.

'On the Gap Left After Leaving'. *Stand*, Vol. 8, No. 2 (1966).
   Killop: i.e. Killhope, in the Northern Pennines, where MacSweeney spent his summers in childhood. Home today of the North of England Lead Mining Museum.

'Walk'. *Stand*, Vol. 8, No. 2 (1966)
   Tynemouth Priory: Ruined 11th Century Benedictine Priory.
   w*illeks*: i.e. whelks.

'The Track, Fervour'. Dated June 4 1967.
   Rimbaud and Verlaine: During their stay in London in 1872, Rimbaud and Paul Verlaine (1844–96) attended a meeting of exiled communards at the Hibernia Store pub on Compton St, Soho.

'Sealine'. Dated June 20 1967.

'Bladder Wrack Blues'. Dated July 20 1967.

'A Letter, This Far Away, Tonight For Liberty'. Dated June 1967. Reprinted in *Tribune*, 18 October 1968.
   Benno Ohnesorg: university student who was killed by police during a demonstration in West Berlin, June 2 1967. His death was of major significance for the extra-parliamentary left in West Germany.

'One Year Old, The Wilted Hybrid'. Dated June 26 1967.
   gin distillery: the Gilbey's gin distillery in Harlow, Essex, where MacSweeney studied journalism 1966–67. Designed by architects Peter Falconer and John Timpson, demolished in the 1990s.

'& The Biggest Bridge is Forty Feet Long'. Dated June 25 1967.
   Biggest Bridge: possibly the crossing of the River Stort at Burntmill Lock, next to Harlow Town railway station.
   it could be 1926: i.e., the British General Strike of 1926.

'On the Burning Down of the Salvation Army Mens Palace'. Dated July 20 1967. Reprinted in *Wolf Tongue*.

'The Axe'. Dated July 21 1967.

'The Boy from the Green Cabaret Tells of His Mother'. Dated August 1967.
   Title: Rimbaud's stay in Charleroi while travelling through Belgium in 1870 is recorded in the sonnet 'Au Cabaret-Vert'.

'The Copper Heart'. Dated July 19 1967.

'City'. Dated July 20 1967.

'Song'. Dated July 1967.

'Pastoral'. Dated July 31 1967.

'The Decision, Finally (for Jeremy Prynne)'. *The English Intelligencer*, Vol. 2, No. 2 (1967).
> *Jeremy Prynne*: J.H. Prynne (1938–), poet, with whom MacSweeney organised the 1967 Sparty Lea Poetry Festival, taking place over Easter and involving a dozen or so poets. MacSweeney published Prynne's *Fire Lizard* (1972); Prynne typeset MacSweeney's *Pearl* (1995), and spoke at his funeral.

From: ***Our Mutual Scarlet Boulevard*** (London: Fulcrum, 1971).

'Map, where the year ends'. *The English Intelligencer*, Vol 1, No. 15 (February 1967).

'For the honour of things, undone'. *The English Intelligencer*, Vol. 2, No. 2 (April 1967).
> *from Essex out*: allusion to 'From Gloucester Out', and 'Idaho Out' by American poet Edward Dorn (1929–99), then resident at the University of Essex. The poem describes the journey from Essex to Sparty Lea.

'The decision'. *The English Intelligencer*, Vol. 2, No. 2 (April 1967).

'Saffron Walden Blues, at the Pond House'. Reprinted in *Antaeus*, No. 2 (1971).
> *Lindisfarne*: also known as Holy Island, situated off the North-East coast of England, and centre of 6th and 7th Century Christianity in the North of England. Home to Saints Aidan and Cuthbert, and visited by Bede.
> *Villon*: François Villon, 15th Century French poet and convict, memorably translated in the 1970s by MacSweeney's friend Stephen Rodefer (1940–2015). MacSweeney frequently alludes to the form of Villon's 'Testament' and 'Legacy' around this time, most notably in his long poem 'The Last Bud'.
> *Chillingham Bull*: breed of wild cattle from Northumberland.

'Six Sonnets for Nathaniel Swift'. *Curiously Strong*, Vol. 2, No. 3 (1969). Also issued in an edition of 25 handmade copies by Blacksuede Boot Press, 1969.
> *Nathaniel Swift*: Unclear, but possibly the Nathaniel Swift of 1860s Cape Cod, whose name is attached to a number of historical houses in Massachusetts. MacSweeney visited the United States in 1969 on a reading tour for *The Boy from the Green Cabaret*.
> *Fred is writing poems*: Fred Buck, American poet, first editor of *The Curiously Strong* in Cambridge, UK, and later *Bezoar* in Gloucester, MA. He writes

about the pollock fish in 'Where the Line Breaks Outward', published in Nick Kimberley's little magazine *Big Venus* (1969). It's possible the other names in the poem (Gary, Jack, etc) refer to other contributors to magazines, but this is speculation.
Meditations: 1966 LP by the John Coltrane sextet, a definitive work of free jazz. *'The Forbidden Pictures'... Emil's labor... Ungemalte Bilder*: Title of an exhibition of watercolours by the German-Danish Expressionist Emil Nolde (1867–1956) held at the Marlborough Gallery, London.
de Chirico's painting: Giorgio de Chirico (1888–1978), Italian artist and writer. The painting's full title is *Mystery and Melancholy of a Street (Girl Running With a Hoop)*.

Poem: 'to belong outside this catastrophe'. *H&* (1970).
no City, nor Cornfield: from William Blake, *Vala, or the Four Zoas*.
Bruno: This is obscure. Blake sometimes rode a pony called Bruno. A more elaborate possibility is the title character of Lewis Carroll's *Sylvie and Bruno*, a child who navigates a world of poets, professors, meteorologists, and many other fantastic types.

'Six Street Songs'. *Curiously Strong*, Vol 2, No. 9 (1970).
Verlaine grumbling...: A fascicle of MacSweeney's translations of Verlaine, titled *Birds in the Night: Poems from the French of Paul Verlaine*, dated September 1967, is in the MacSweeney papers at Newcastle University.
Mallarmé: Stéphane Mallarmé (1842–1898), French poet, whose unfinished elegy for his son Anatole was first published in 1961.

From: ***Flames on the Beach at Viareggio*** (London: Blacksuede Boot, 1970).

'England is bonny in May but small'. *Big Venus*, No. 4 (1970)
"Two Pieces": Frank O'Hara, *Two Pieces* (London: Long Hair Books, 1969). Contains 'Commercial Variations' and 'Those Who Are Dreaming', both of which are echoed in MacSweeney's poem.
Léger's brassy men: Fernand Léger (1881–1955), French painter and sculptor.

'the great and tragic bouquet of life'. *Amazing Grace*, No. 1 (1970)
The opening line is a translation of a line from Laforgue's 'Rosace en Vitrail': 'Alors, le grand bouquet tragique de la Vie!'

'Lost is the Day'. Printed as a New Year's Day greetings broadside by the bookseller Larry Walrich, 1971.

12 Poems & a Letter. *Curiously Strong*, Vol. 4, Nos. 3–4 (1971), appearing as the B-side to MacSweeney's *Just 22 and I Don't Mind Dyin'*.

Elaine Randell: poet, editor of *Amazing Grace* magazine and Secret Books. Married MacSweeney in 1973; separated in 1979. Helped MacSweeney edit the Blacksuede Boot Press. This appears to be their only published collaboration.

Fools Gold (London: Blacksuede Boot, 1972).
Reprinted in *The Tempers of Hazard* (1993). The text here follows the later printing in *ToH*, which makes minor emendations to the punctuation.
   Aberglaube: German for 'superstition'. Matthew Arnold, in *Literature and Dogma* (1873) translates it as 'extra-belief', that is, 'belief beyond what is certain or verifiable'. He cites Goethe: '*Aberglaube* is the poetry of life.'

Dance Steps (Kent: Joe DiMaggio 1972).
   tagore: Rabindranath Tagore (1861–1941). Bengali poet and writer, winner of 1913 Nobel Prize for Literature.
   Goethe/Werther: Johann Wolfgang von Goethe (1749–1832), poet, writer, scientist, author of *The Sorrows of Young Werther* (1744).
   "piper at the Gates of Dawn": Pink Floyd LP (1967), featuring the song 'Take Up Thy Stethoscope and Walk', referenced here.
   John Betjeman: Betjeman (1906–84) was made Poet Laureate of the United Kingdom after the death of C. Day Lewis in May 1972.

Toad Church (1972).
Sections 11, 12, 13, *Turpin*, No. 4 (1974). Published in full for the first time in *Chicago Review* 59:3 (2015), with a brief commentary by Luke Roberts. The text is based on a typescript dated December 1972, held at Newcastle University Special Collections.
   bust / of Nelson: a bronze bust of Horatio Nelson (1758–1805) stands in the National Maritime Museum in Greenwich, London. MacSweeney worked at the Museum in 1972 as a conservator of paintings.
   Carmichael: John Carmichael (1800–68), Newcastle-born maritime painter.
   Everett: John Everett (1876–1949): English maritime painter. MacSweeney's 'Homage to John Everett' is collected in *Wolf Tongue*.
   Bing Crosby: American singer and light entertainer. Died 1977.
   Horbiger: likely Hanns Hörbiger (1860–1931), Austrian mining engineer and amateur astrologist, whose 'glacial cosmogony' became popular during the Third Reich.
   Waltz Mephisto: the four works known as 'The Mephisto Waltzes' were composed by Franz Liszt between 1859 and 1885. *Mephisto Waltz* was also an American horror film, released in 1971.
   T. Rex: Glam-Rock band, led by Marc Bolan, whose most popular single

'Get It On' was released in 1971.
Jubilate Agno: Ecstatic religious poem written by Christopher Smart while confined in an asylum between 1759 and 1763.
Spinoza: Baruch Spinoza (1632–77), Dutch philosopher.
Messiaen: Olivier Messiaen (1908–92), French composer.
Karenina: The novel *Anna Karenina*, by Leo Tolstoy (1828–1910).

Fog Eye (Brighton: Ted Kavanagh, 1973).
M.H.: Mark Hyatt, poet, who killed himself in summer 1972. MacSweeney published his posthumous book *How Odd* (1973) in collaboration with Andrew Crozier's Ferry Press.

Pelt Feather Log (1974).
Published here for the first time in full. Extracts appear in *Breakfast* (1974) and *Turpin*, Nos. 7–8 (1974). It was also announced in the *Descriptive Catalogue* of the Grosseteste Press in 1975, as follows: 'A sequence of 23 poems firmly based in a series of sensual particularities but dealing not just with topography or with the history of a sensibility: the inner & the outer geographies are, in every sense, at once, "related".' The text in this volume is based on the final of three typescripts of the work in progress sent by MacSweeney to J.H. Prynne in 1973–74.

Macpherson Collection: Large collection of prints in the National Maritime Museum.
Millwall Dock: MacSweeney's Father's family were from the Isle of Dogs, East London. Millwall Dock is just across the river from the Maritime Museum in Greenwich.
emva cream: Emva Cream is a brand of fortified wine.
Crow Pool...Hangman's Hill: areas in Allenheads.

Starry Messenger (Kent: Secret Books 1980).
The poem was composed in 1975, and initially published in *Pod* magazine in 1976. The text is based on the Secret Books printing.

Black Torch (London: New London Pride, 1978).
Extracts in *Polymnia*, Vol. 1, No. 1 (1975), *Great Works*, No. 5 (1975), *Bezoar*, Vol. 2, No. 2 (1975), and *Square One* (1977). 'Black Torch Sunrise' appeared in *Poetry Review*, Vol. 67, Nos. 1–2 (1977), and was subsequently printed in *Wolf Tongue*. The text here follows the New London Pride edition.

In a prose preface which accompanied the material in *Bezoar*, MacSweeney wrote:
    "*Black Torch Strike* is a political and geographical sequence drawing

on the history of the miners' struggles against low wages, long hours and abysmal working conditions in the coal mines of Northumberland and Durham in North East England. The place where radical left-wing socialism grew up alongside the radicalism of free-thinking preachers – where each man who could read carried a copy of John Bunyan's *Pilgrim's Progress*; those who couldn't formed their own "ranter's" schools and took their wives and bairns to original working-class schools. Ranters were the free-thinking, whose Devil was the Boss and the Pit-Owner, whose Heaven was workers' controlled pits. These particular sections are from a sequence whose source is the Durham Miners' Strike of 1844. The men were locked out of work for six months for demanding improved conditions. Eventually driven out of their homes by bailiffs backed by King's Militia, they lived in earth houses on the bitter-cold Durham Moors, feeding themselves on nettles and grass. The strike was lost as blacklegs were 'imported' from other parts of Britain for wages higher than those demanded by the Durhamites. But it laid a tough foundation which still makes the National Union of Mineworkers the strongest most radical union in the land. Ask Edward Heath. They toppled his Tory Government in May, 1973. The sequence is written partly phonetically, in the Northumbrian dialect."

Throughout *Black Torch*, MacSweeney draws from the following books, in both marked and unmarked quotations:
  R.J. Charleton, *History of Newcastle Upon Tyne, from the Earliest Records to its Formation as a City in 1882* (1895)
  Friedrich Engels, *The Condition of the Working Class in England* (1845)
  E.P. Thompson, *The Making of the English Working Class* (1963)
  The Report of the Children's Employment Commission (1842)

'Prologue'.
  Eric Mottram (1924–95): Poet and academic. Edited *Poetry Review* 1971–77. Interview with MacSweeney in *Poetry Information*, No. 18. MacSweeney published his *Homage to Braque* (1976), and Mottram's *A Faithful Private* (1976) is dedicated to MacSweeney.

'Black Torch'.
  Tom and Connie: Tom and Connie Pickard.
  Halfden: Presumably the Viking Halfdan Ragnarsson, whose army invaded the Kingdom of Northumbria in the 9th Century.
  Ida: Ida of Bernicia, whose grandson Aethelfrith became first King of Northumbria in the early 7th Century.
  dog-eyed Pearl: The first appearance of the character Pearl, who would become central to MacSweeney's writing in the 1990s.

Dan Smith: T. Dan Smith (1915–93), Labour politician, oversaw redevelopment of Newcastle city centre as head of council, 1960–65. Engulfed by corruption scandals involving the architect John Poulson, sentenced to prison in 1974, released 1977.
Alderman Cunningham: Andrew Cunningham (1910–2010), prominent within the Labour Party and Trade Union movement in the North-East. Sentenced to prison in 1974, released 1976.

'Black Lamp Strike'.
Marcus Despard: Edward Marcus Despard (1751–1803), Irish soldier, member of the London Corresponding Society, executed for the alleged 'Despard Plot', a plan to assassinate King George III.
Jeremiah Brandreth (1785–1817): Foiled Luddite revolutionary, executed for treason.
Flower's marauders: Benjamin Flower (1755–1829), English radical journalist, acquaintance of Samuel Taylor Coleridge, editor of the seditious *The Cambridge Intelligencer*.
Paine: Thomas Paine (1737–1809), American-English revolutionary, author of *The Rights of Man, The Age of Reason*, and *Agrarian Justice*.

'Black Torch Sunrise'
Ginsberg: Allen Ginsberg (1926–97), legendary American poet, friend of Tom Pickard and Basil Bunting. His visit to England in 1965 was seen by some as the beginning of the British Poetry Revival. Epigraph from 'Ecologue', in *The Fall of America: Poems of These States, 1965–71* (1973).
TUC: The Trades Union Congress, which in 1978 sided with the management during the Grunwick Dispute.
Sir John Gielgud (1904–2000): English actor. 'At Three Minutes Past Eight You Must Dream' is the title of a *New Yorker* profile by Kenneth Tynan of the actor Ralph Richardson, who starred with Gielgud in Harold Pinter's play *No Man's Land* on Broadway, February 1977.
Lee J Cobb (1910–76): American film star. Appeared in *On the Waterfront* (1954) as a corrupt union boss. Testified to the House Un-American Activities in 1953, naming 20 ex-members of the Communist Party USA.
Sal Mineo (1939–76): American actor. Appeared in *Rebel Without a Cause* (1955).
John Martin (1789–1854): Painter and engineer, born in Haydon Bridge, about ten miles north of Sparty Lea. Designed a Miner's Lamp and a system of ventilation. The Laing Gallery in Newcastle holds a large collection of his works.

Jury Vet Told: Come Back and Learn the Way
First published in *Slow Dancer*, No. 7 (1980). The textual layout of the first three

stanzas of 'Into the Dangerous Decade' has been slightly modified for typographical reasons.

'Ode Antique Tongue'.
Herrick: epigraph from 'Upon the Nipples of Julia's Breast', Robert Herrick (1591–1674).

'Carve Her Name With Pride'.
Title: 1958 film starring Virginia Mckenna based on the life of French wartime hero Violette Szabo.
Aella's Bride: See Chatterton's 'Aella: A Tragycall Enterlude'.

Blood Money
First published in *Slow Dancer*, Nos. 12–13 (1983).
This is one of two uncollected poems MacSweeney wrote titled 'Blood Money'. The more substantial is the later unpublished sonnet sequence, *Blood Money: The Marvellous Secret Sonnets of Mary Bell, Child-Killer*.

NEDC: National Economic Development Council.
Reggie Maudling: Reginald Maudling (1917–79), Conservative politician, was involved in the Poulson/T. Dan Smith scandals. He persuaded the Government of Malta to award the contract for hospital construction to John Poulson's architecture firm.
JackJim...: Presumably the names of Labour Party Council members.

Revulsion (1985)
Previously unpublished. Copies held in typescript at the University of Newcastle, and in the Eric Mottram Collection at King's College London. The text here is based on the Mottram copy.
Title: Jayne Torvill and Christopher Dean, British figure-skating duo. They won gold medals at the 1984 Winter Olympics.
Meat Puppets: American psychedelic punk band. Their most popular record, *Meat Puppets II* was released in 1984.
Black Flag: American hardcore punk band.
Fancy Dan: T. Dan Smith
Natalie Wood (1938–81): American actor, appeared in *Rebel Without a Cause* and *West Side Story* (1961). Drowned during a boating trip.

Soft Hail (1988)
Previously unpublished. An extract appeared in *I Mag* (1990). Copy held in type-

script at the University of Newcastle, which I have followed here.
Hadrian: Roman Emperor, whose wall across the North of England marked the limit of the Roman Empire. There's an exposed section of the Wall in Denton Burn, where MacSweeney lived.
Büchner's Lenz: 'Lenz' is an unfinished story by Georg Büchner (1813–37). Paul Celan (1920–70) comments on it in his speech known as 'The Meridian'.
Boulmer: Village on the North-East coast, one of those featured in the BBC Shipping Forecast.

'Ode: Completely Fragged in this New Dawn'
Printed, with short prose comment by MacSweeney, in *High On the Walls: A Morden Tower Anthology*, ed. by Gordon Brown (Newcastle: Bloodaxe, 1990).

From: *Hellhound Memos* (The Many Press, 1993).
The other poems from the sequence appear in *Wolf Tongue*.

'Your tentship'
Mary: see John Clare, 'To Mary'.

'Sky so very vast and blue'.
B&Q: Chain of English 'home improvement' DIY shops, expanded rapidly in the 1980s.

'Hellhound Rapefield Memo'.
Crypt of St Mary Redcliffe: the church in Bristol where Chatterton supposedly discovered the Rowley manuscripts.
Anne Sexton (1928–74): American poet, influence on *Hellhound Memos* and the later *Book of Demons*. She killed herself in 1974.
Robert Johnson (1911–38): Legendary American bluesman. According to legend, made a pact with the devil at the crossroads in order to acquire his extraordinary gift.

'So quiet tonight'.
Christina Catherine Fraser-Tytler (1848–1927). English mystical poet. The quotation comes from her anthology-piece, 'In Summer Fields'.
Arizona Dranes (1891–1963): American gospel singer, whose Okeh Recordings were made 1926–1929.

'Rachel, darkness'.
Rachel Bierley: Daughter of the journalist Stephen Bierley, whom Mac-

Sweeney describes in *Pearl* as 'best friend of Barry'.
Betty Blue: 1986 French feature film about a woman's descent into madness.

'Garbled Manifest'.
Bladerunner-style: The sci-fi film *Blade Runner*, directed by Ridley Scott (1937–), who was born in South Shields.

'Jerusalem has been sold'.
Hildegard of Bingen: 12th Century Christian mystic, composer. The epigraph is from her *Book of Divine Works*.
Tempest Vane: Vane Tempest is a colliery in Durham, last working shift in October 1992.
Mercantile Dry Dock: A shipyard in Jarrow, on the river Tyne.

'The malevolent honeyblack'.
Emily Brontë (1819–1848): English novelist and poet. The epigraph comes from 'The Visionary', which is in *The Penguin Anthology of Mystical Verse* alongside Fraser-Tytler.

From: ***Postcards from Hitler*** (London: Writers Forum, 1988)
The title sequence is reprinted in *Wolf Tongue*. Some of the spacing between the sections has been reduced, and some spellings have been corrected.

'I am Lucifer'.
Tony Blair (1953–): leader of the Labour Party from 1994, became Prime Minister in 1997. As the spearhead of 'New Labour' he represented a break with socialism in the Parliamentary Labour Party. His local constituency as an MP was Sedgefield, Durham.
Harriet Harman (1950–): Labour MP, Secretary of State for Social Security in Blair's first government.
Neil boy: Presumably Neil Kinnock (1942–), leader of the Labour Party from 1983 to his election defeat in 1992.
Jim Burns (1936–): Preston-born poet, contributor to *The English Intelligencer*. He reviewed books for the left-Labour newspaper *Tribune* in the 1960s and 1970s, including work by MacSweeney. Edited *Palantir* magazine, which published work by MacSweeney.
Moscow Dynamo: Soviet football team, who played a friendly with Newcastle United in 1965.
Yevgeny: Yevgeny Yevtushenko (1932–2017), Soviet poet who came to prominence in the West in the 1960s. MacSweeney was a particular fan of his *A Precocious Autobiography* (1963).
Vivienne of Hammer Horror: Vivienne Carlton, MacSweeney's girlfriend in the late 1960s, who appears briefly in the Hammer Horror film, *The Curse of*

the Crimson Altar (1968).
Keld or Reeth: Villages in North Yorkshire.
Urthely: Pearl, 'for urthely herte might not suffyse'.
Andy Cole (1971–): Striker and top goalscorer for Newcastle United from 1993 until his shock transfer to arch-rivals Manchester United in 1995.
Kevin Keegan (1951–): Manager of Newcastle United, 1992–1997. Took Newcastle to the brink of Premier League victory during the 1995–96 season. Resigned from the club in January 1997.
Alan Shearer (1970–): Striker, signed for Newcastle in 1996. Struggled with injuries during the 1997–98 season.
Bruce Willis (1955–): American action-film actor, famous for the *Die Hard* series.

'My Former Darling Country'
Title: compare George Orwell's essay, 'My Country Right or Left' (1940).
Arthur: Presumably Arthur Scargill (1938–), head of the National Union of Mineworkers during the 1984–85 miners' strike.
Dusty Springfield (1939–99): English singer, subject of an unfinished collaboration between Barry MacSweeney and Nick Pemberton called *Island of Dreams* (c. 1998).
Carl Wilson (1946–98): American musician, member of the Beach Boys, died February 1998.
Colin Sandwich: A British television sitcom called *Colin's Sandwich* ran for two series between 1988–1990, about a British Rail employee who hoped to find success as a horror writer.
Johnny Rotten: John Lydon (1956–), lead singer of The Sex Pistols and Public Image Limited.
Lenin: Born Vladimir Ilyich Ulyanov, Lenin (1870–1923) was leader of the Bolshevik faction of the Russian Social Democratic Party. The key theoretician of the Russian Revolution.
Mayakovsky: Vladimir Mayakovsky (1893–1930), Bolshevik poet. Died by suicide in 1930.
George Barker (1913–81): English poet, contemporary of Dylan Thomas. His 1937 *Calamiterror* is a lost classic of the Spanish Civil War.
Francis Thompson (1859–1907): English mystical poet, most famous for 'The Hound of Heaven' (1893).

From: ***Horses in Boiling Blood*** (Cambridge: Equipage 2003)
The text here is based on the Equipage printing, with some minor corrections of type, and some changes to the typography.

'War Roses'.
Marquis de Sade: Apollinaire edited a selection of Sade's writings in 1909.

'Troubled Are These Times'.
    Esmerelda: the character from Victor Hugo's *The Hunchback of Notre Dame*.
    Elvet swanne: Elvet is an area of Durham City. The name is derived from the Old English for 'swan'.
    Mrs Goebbels: Magda Goebbels (1901–45), prominent Nazi and wife of Propaganda Minister Joseph Goebbels.
    Dr Mengele: Josef Mengele (1911–79), Nazi, physician at Auschwitz.
    Jacqueline: Jackie, or S.J. Litherland, poet, and partner of MacSweeney in the 1990s. Also Jacqueline Kolb, who married Apollinaire in 1918.
    Joan Miró (1893–1983): Spanish painter and visual artist, acquaintance of Apollinaire.
    Bob Dylan (1941–): American singer and writer, an early and enduring influence on MacSweeney.
    Emmylou Harris (1947–): American country singer. Contributed extensively to Bob Dylan's *Desire* LP (1975).
    Septre 6e 1997: date of the funeral of Diana, Princess of Wales, who was killed in a car accident in Paris on August 31 1997.

'Feast of Fashion Burning Down: Zone'.
    Esenin: Sergei Esenin (1895–1925), Russian poet, killed himself in 1925.
    Pacino: Al Pacino (1940–), American actor with distinctive accent.
    Jeremy Beadle: Beadle (1948–2008) was an English TV presenter, known for practical jokes.
    Enoch of Birmingham: Enoch Powell (1912–98), Conservative politician remembered for his racist 'Rivers of Blood' speech given in 1968.
    Bobby Sands (1954–81): Irish Republican, interned in Long Kesh Prison. He was elected as Member of Parliament while on Hunger Strike in 1981, and died a month later.
    Corstopitum: Roman town in the North-East of England, near modern-day Corbridge.

'Terrible Changes'.
    Bigg Market: Area of Newcastle famous for raucous nightlife.
    Fenwick's: Large department store in Newcastle city centre, founded 1882.
    Turks Head: The Royal Turk's Head Hotel on Grey St, Newcastle.
    Hellhound Trail Tour: A reading tour MacSweeney took with Nicholas Johnson in 1997.

'Victory Over Darkness & The Sunne'.
    Title: *Victory Over the Sun* is a Russian Futurist opera, premiered in 1913 with contributions by Khlebnikov and Malevich.
    Tatlin: Vladimir Tatlin (1885–1963), Soviet architect, designer of the unbuilt *Monument to the Third International*.

Malevich (1878–1934): Kazimir Malevich, Russian painter.
Corelli: Arcangelo Corelli (1653–1713), Italian baroque composer.
Handel: George Frideric Handel (1685–1759), German British composer. Influenced by Corelli.
Herald of Free Enterprise: passenger ferry which sank in Zeebrugge, Belgium, in 1987 killing 193.
Simon Armitage (1963–): English poet, prominent contributor the English GCSE curriculum.
Kerouac's Big Sur: Jack Kerouac (1922–69), American poet and novelist. *Big Sur* (1962) dealt extensively with Kerouac's alcoholism.

'Cornflower'.
Elaine: Elaine Randell.
Ray Davidson: Unknown.

'Cold Mountain Ode'.
Why Should I Be Lonely: 'Why Should I Be Lonely', country song by Jimmie Rodgers, first recorded 1930. MacSweeney refers to the version by Aaron Neville recorded for a Jimmie Rodgers tribute LP in 1997.
Cheaneys / Grensons: English footwear manufacturers.
Bill dead Allen Gone is Ed dead: William S. Burroughs died August 2 1997; Allen Ginsberg died April 5 1997; Edward Dorn was diagnosed with inoperable cancer in May 1997.
Snyder: Gary Snyder (1930–), American beat poet and ecological activist. Translated the 'Cold Mountain' poems of 8th Century Chinese poet Han Shan.

'Sam Arrives to Take Grandad for Dawn Tickling'.
Sam: Sammy the Poacher.
Grandad: See MacSweeney's elegy for Gordon Calvert, *Blackbird*.

'Memories Are Made of This'.
Garth Hudson (1937–): Member of The Band. 'Tears of Rage', written by Bob Dylan, is the opening track to The Band's 1968 record *The Big Pink*.
Milhaud's Four Seasons: Darius Milhaud (1892–1974), French modernist composer. Poulenc's opera, *Les Mamelles de Tirésias* (1945), based on Apollinaire's play of the same name, is dedicated to Milhaud.
Pablo: Pablo Picasso (1881–1973), artist, friend of Guillaume Apollinaire.

'Love's Swanne Song'.
Symphonie Phantastique: Hector Berlioz, *Symphonie fantastique* (1830).

'The Illegal 2CV'.
Kev: Unknown. Possibly a fantasy of Newcastle United manager, Kevin

Keegan, known as 'King Kev'.
Carliol Place: Site of NHS Specialist Mental Health Services for Drug and Alcohol addiction in Newcastle.

'At the Hoppings'.
Title: The Hoppings is an annual funfair, held on the Town Moor, Newcastle.
Hellhound Train Never Ending Tour: A reading tour undertaken by MacSweeney and Nicholas Johnson in 1997.

'I Don't Walk the Line'.
the fall: Possible reference to English post-punk band The Fall.
A bonus like rain: cf. the title of Jackie Litherland's 2010 collection, *The Absolute Bonus of Rain*.

'All of Your Sinnes'.
Lou: Louise de Coligny-Châtillon (1881–1963), Apollinaire's lover, subject of many of the early poems in *Calligrammes*. Apollinaire often puns on her name, transforming it into *loup*, i.e. *wolf*, a move that would surely appeal to MacSweeney.

'Petition to the Jesus Christ Almighty'.
Black Middens: particularly hazardous rock formation at the mouth of the Tyne.
NUS: National Union of Seamen.

'Entrance to Heaven'.
Neptune Yard: shipyard in Wallsend, Tyneside. Incorporated into Swan Hunter, closed 1988.

'Listen It's Plutting'.
Title: 'Plutting', Northern dialect for a light rain.
Club A'Gogo: Newcastle R&B music venue. The Animals recorded a live LP, 'In the Beginning' at the club in 1963.
Muddy Waters (1913–83): Legendary American blues musician.
Jimmy Reed (1925–76): Legendary American blues musician, who wrote the much-covered 'Bright Lights Big City'.
Elba: Italian island where Napoleon I was exiled in 1814. The line 'I am France and France is Me' is sometimes attributed to Napoleon.

'Letter From Guillaume'.
Rookwood Road: street near to MacSweeney's house in Denton Burn.

'1997'.
 Stephen says: The American poet Stephen Rodefer (1940–2015), who lived in Paris.

'Rue Christine Lundi'.
 Loaning Head: isolated area just above Alston in the North Pennines.
 Rachel Levitas: Daughter of Jackie Litherland, whose painting *Temptation of St Anthony II* appears on the front cover of MacSweeney's *The Book of Demons*.

'Lou's the name'.
 Rouveyre: André Rouveyre, French writer, dear friend of Guillaume Apollinaire. He collaborated with Henri Matisse on a biography of Apollinaire published in 1952.
 Epinal / Georgin: Épinal was a centre of French printmaking in the late 18th to the mid-19th Century. François Georgin was a popular illustrator in the early 19th Century.

Letters to Dewey.
First published in *Sweet Advocate* (Cambridge: Equipage, 2000). The text follows the Equipage publication, but I have regularised the titles.
Title: Dewey Rodefer is the son of the late Stephen Rodefer, whom MacSweeney visited in Paris, 1997.
 Serbs: The Kosovo War ended in June 1999.
 B-52s: American New-Wave band.
 Zane Grey (1872–1939): American author of Westerns.
 John Duncan (1866–1945): Scottish painter, whose *St Bride* (1913) hangs in the Scottish National Gallery.
 Buddy Holly (1936–59): American rock'n'roll singer and musician.
 James Brown (1933–2006): American singer, funk musician, Godfather of soul.
 Lay your heart: Matthew 6:19–21: 'Lay not up for yourselves treasures upon the earth, where moth and rust doth corrupt, and where thieves break through and steal: But lay up for yourselves treasures in heaven, where neither moth nor rust doth corrupt, and where thieves do not break through nor steal: For where your treasure is, there will be your heart also.'

False Lapwing (Cambridge: Poetical Histories, 2002).
Peter Riley (1940–), editor of Poetical Histories, friend and supporter of MacSweeney, notes of the typescript on which the publication is based:

> 'After the last line of False Lapwing the following occurs after a 3-line space—"burn them burn them burn them But save the best", which

I have removed as I don't believe it is a part of the poem, but rather an apostrophe addressed to the world, or posterity, or possibly me. Other than that, only a few keyboarding errors have been corrected. […] Under False Lapwing is typed "BPM 2000 for Peter Riley 60". Under Pearl Standing … is typed "BPM 2000 Inspired by Pierre Reverdy. Happy Birthday Peter".'

The title is from Chaucer's *Parlement of Foules*: 'the false lapwynge, full of trecherye'.

Index of Titles

12 Poems and a Letter	63
1997	296
A Letter, This Far Away, Tonight for Liberty	28
All Of Your Sinnes Will be Known Always And Never Forgiven	285
& The Biggest Bridge is Forty Feet Long	30
Annie	287
At The Hoppings	281
Autobiography of Barry MacSweeney	21
The Axe	32
Black Lamp Strike	167
Black Torch	141
Black Torch	137
Black Torch Sunrise	169
Bladder Wrack Blues	27
Blood Money	184
The Boy from the Green Cabaret Tells of His Mother	19
The Boy from the Green Cabaret Tells of His Mother	33
Carve Her Name With Pride	181
City	35
Cold Mountain Ode	270
The Copper Heart	34
Cornflower	268
Dance Steps	79
The decision	44
The Decision, Finally (for Jeremy Prynne) 4 a.m., March 24 Sparty Lea	37
The DollBird/Redblonde	289
Elegy	100
'England is bonny in May but small'	57
Entrance to Heaven	288
False Lapwing	319
False Lapwing	317
Feast of Fashion Burning Down: Zone	254
Flames on the Beach at Viareggio	55
Fog Eye	103
Fog Eye	97

The Folded Man	99
Fools Gold	71
For the honour of things, undone	43
Forget About Her She Does Not Exist	279
Future Dream	102
Garbled Manifest – No Hellhole Unturned	223
The Garden Door is Open On The World	277
'the great and tragic bouquet of life'	58
Hellhound Rapefield Memo	220
Hellhound Memos	217
Horses in Boiling Blood	245
I Don't Walk the Line All of the Time	283
I am Lucifer	229
The Illegal 2CV	275
Into the Dangerous Decade	177
'Jerusalem has been sold'	224
Jury Vet Told: Come Back & Learn the Way	177
Letter From Guillaume Apollinaire to Barry MacSweeney	294
Letters to Dewey	307
Listen It's Plutting	292
Lost is the Day	59
Lou's the Name on My Lips	303
Love Song	101
Love's Swanne Song	274
'The malevolent honeyblack'	225
Map, where the year ends	41
Melrose to South Shields	163
Memories Are Made of This	273
My Former Darling Country Wrong or Wrong	241
Ode Antique Tongue	179
Ode to Snowe	263
Ode: 'Completely Fragged in this New Dawn'	216
On the Burning Down of the Salvation Army Men's Palace	31
On the Gap Left After Leaving	23
One Year Old, The Wilted Hybrid	29
Our Mutual Scarlet Boulevard	39

Pastoral	36
Pearl Standing Alone in Sparty Moonlight	321
Pelt Feather Log	109
Petition to the Jesus Christ Almighty	286
Poem: 'to belong outside this catastrophe'	51
Postcards from Hitler	227
Prologue: Iron & Bread	139
'Rachel, darkness'	322
Revulsion	188
Rue Christine Lundi	298
Saffron Walden Blues, at the Pond House	45
Sam Arrives to Take Grandad for the Dawn Tickling	272
Sealine	27
2nd Telephone Song	36
Secret Poem Number Nine	295
Six Sonnets For Nathaniel Swift	48
Six Street Songs	52
'Sky so very vast and blue'	219
'So quiet tonight'	221
Soft Hail	197
Song	35
Starry Messenger	133
Terrible Changes	261
To Lynn at Work whose Surname I don't know	22
To Me Mam, Somewhere to the North of This Shit	38
Toad Church	85
The Track, Fervour	26
Treasure	300
Troubled Are These Times	249
'underground carpark in the rain'	58
Victory Over Darkness & The Sunne	264
Walk	24
War Roses	247
'Your tentship, your azureness, your cornflower'	219

www.ingramcontent.com/pod-product-compliance
Lightning Source LLC
Chambersburg PA
CBHW022000160426
43197CB00007B/209